WHAT PRINCIPALS NEED TO KNOW ABOUT
Teaching and Learning Science

SECOND EDITION

ERIC C. SHENINGER

KEITH DEVEREAUX

A Joint Publication — Solution Tree / naesp

Copyright © 2013 by Solution Tree Press

Materials appearing here are copyrighted. With one exception, all rights are reserved. Readers may reproduce only those pages marked "Reproducible." Otherwise, no part of this book may be reproduced or transmitted in any form or by any means (electronic, photocopying, recording, or otherwise) without prior written permission of the publisher.

555 North Morton Street
Bloomington, IN 47404
800.733.6786 (toll free) / 812.336.7700
FAX: 812.336.7790

email: info@solution-tree.com
solution-tree.com

Visit **go.solution-tree.com/leadership** to download the reproducibles in this book.

Printed in the United States of America

16 15 14 13 12   1 2 3 4 5

Library of Congress Cataloging-in-Publication Data

Sheninger, Eric C.
  What principals need to know about teaching and learning science / Eric C. Sheninger, Keith Devereaux. -- 2nd ed.
       p. cm.
    Includes bibliographical references and index.
    ISBN 978-1-935543-58-9 (perfect bound) 1. Science--Study and teaching (Elementary)--United States. 2. Science--Study and teaching (Middle school)--United States. 3. Elementary school principals--United States--Handbooks, manuals, etc. 4. Middle school principals--United States--Handbooks, manuals, etc. I. Devereaux, Keith. II. Title.
   LB1585.3.S55 2012
   372.35'044--dc23
                                                                            2012023098

Solution Tree
Jeffrey C. Jones, CEO
Edmund M. Ackerman, President

Solution Tree Press
President: Douglas M. Rife
Publisher: Robert D. Clouse
Editorial Director: Lesley Bolton
Managing Production Editor: Caroline Wise
Senior Production Editor: Edward Levy
Copy Editor: Sarah Payne-Mills
Proofreader: Elisabeth Abrams
Text Designer: Jenn Taylor
Cover Designer: Amy Shock

ACKNOWLEDGMENTS

A book like this would not be possible without the profound influence of passionate science educators. Influential teachers instilled Eric's interest in and enthusiasm for science at a young age—teachers like Wayne South, whose quirkiness, commitment to working with students outside of school, and innovative approach to project-based learning fueled his passion for this subject; high school chemistry teacher Raymond Hynoski, whose caring nature and belief in his students were the catalysts that led Eric to pursue a science degree in college; and Salisbury University professor Dr. Judith Stribling, who not only pushed his thinking but made trudging through the wetlands of the Eastern Shore of Maryland fun. From an educational leadership perspective, Eric is grateful for many key influencers and pillars of support. His parents—Arthur and Jean Sheninger—as well as his professors at East Stroudsburg University—Faith Waters, Doug Lare, Patricia Smeaton, and Kathleen Foster—who provided him with the tools, confidence, and desire to be a high school principal. Finally, Eric is deeply grateful for the support he receives from the New Milford board of education, administration, high school staff, and community.

Educators have had a profound influence on Keith as well and have led him into his profession. Ray Digrazia not only truly inspired him to pursue a degree in biology but also showed him the effect a passionate educator could have on a student. Other teachers, like Jon Noschese and James Wilson, taught him that a teacher could be funny yet effective in his or her teaching practices. Coaches like the late Steven Konde helped shape Keith's character. Further thanks go to the professors of Richard Stockton College—Tim Haresign, Kelly Keenan, and Rich Hager—for continuing to fuel his passion for science—and to others like Tara Crowell and Kristine Maul for helping to polish his communication tools, enabling him to become a more effective educator. Keith would like to thank the faculty and staff of New Milford High School for their support and for their continued dedication to the children of that community. Finally, Keith would like to thank his parents, Jack and Leslie Devereaux, for supporting him in everything he has ever wanted to do.

Finally, Eric and Keith would like to thank the staff of Solution Tree, in particular Douglas Rife, who convinced Eric to write this book; Ed Levy, who stayed on top of things throughout the process and was always there to answer questions and provide support; and Sarah Payne-Mills, whose keen eye and sound suggestions greatly assisted in creating this resource.

Solution Tree Press would like to thank the following reviewers:

Subha Balagopal
Principal
Spring Mill Elementary School
Indianapolis, Indiana

Lyn Countryman
Interim Director, Malcolm Price
  Laboratory School
University of Northern Iowa
Cedar Falls, Iowa

Tammie Davenport
Science Teacher
Gifford Middle School
Vero Beach, Florida

Kelly Davis
Principal
Woodbrook Elementary School
Carmel, Indiana

John Lowry
Assistant Principal
Shades Cahaba Elementary School
Homewood, Alabama

Pamela C. Robertson
Principal
Miles Avenue Elementary School
Huntington Park, California

Christine A. Royce
Associate Professor, Department of
  Teacher Education
Shippensburg University
Shippensburg, Pennsylvania

Melissa Sleeper
Science Teacher
Gifford Middle School
Vero Beach, Florida

William Joseph Sumrall Jr.
Professor, Department of Elementary
  Education
University of Mississippi
Oxford, Mississippi

Julie Thomas
Adjunct Instructor, College of Education
Oklahoma State University
Stillwater, Oklahoma

Robert E. Yager
Professor of Science Education
University of Iowa
Iowa City, Iowa

Amanda York
Science Lab Educator
Bremen Fourth and Fifth Grade Academy
Bremen, Georgia

TABLE OF CONTENTS

Reproducible pages are in italics.
Visit **go.solution-tree.com/leadership** to download the reproducibles in this book.

About the Authors ix

INTRODUCTION
Leading Change 1
    Beginning the Process 1
    Professional Development and Science Education 3
    About This Book 3

ONE
Scientific Inquiry 5
    Scientific Methods and Scientific Literacy 6
    A Global Consensus 9
    Summary 14

TWO
Science Curricula 15
    Your School's Science Content 16
    Curricular Alignment 18
    Cognitive Domains 20
    A Further Look at Curricular Materials and Activities 21
    Summary 29

THREE
Science Program Evaluation 31
    Science Program Self-Assessment Survey 31
    Other Data Worth Considering 36
    Summary 37

FOUR
Inquiry-Based Learning 39
    Supporting Teachers in Planning for Science Instruction 40
    Providing Assessment Support 40
    Promoting Inquiry-Based Teaching 42
    Globally Enhancing the Science Classroom 51
    Summary 53

FIVE
Assessment 55
    Assessments to Evaluate Science Learning 57
    The Integration of Authentic Assessment 58
    Summary 65

SIX
Professional Development 67
    Planning a Meaningful Professional Development Program 68
    The Process of Professional Development 69
    Summary 71

APPENDIX A
Reproducibles 73
    Evaluating Science Curricular Materials *74*
    Experimental Design Diagram *76*
    Science Program Self-Assessment Survey *77*
    Reflective Discussion Guidelines *79*
    Planning to Teach for Understanding I *80*
    Planning to Teach for Understanding II *81*
    Direct Observation Inventory *82*
    Indicators of Ineffective Science Instruction *84*
    Observation Guidelines for K–8 Science Classroom Learning Climate *85*
    Observation Guidelines for K–8 Science Teachers *86*
    Observation Guidelines for K–8 Science Students *87*
    Observation Guidelines for K–8 Science Classroom Environment *88*
    Observation Guidelines for K–8 Schoolwide Science Climate *89*
    Assessment Checklist *90*
    Survey for Assessment and Evaluation *92*
    Tracking the Impact of Professional Development *93*

APPENDIX B
Resources for Learning More 95
    Elementary School Resources 95
    Middle School Resources 96
    Technology Resources 97
    Educational Resources 98
    Science Organizations 100

APPENDIX C
State Professional Science Teacher Associations 103

APPENDIX D
Science Content Standards for Inquiry 105
    Fundamental Abilities Necessary to Do Scientific Inquiry 105
    Fundamental Understandings About Scientific Inquiry 106

APPENDIX E
Sample K–2 Science Activity: The Mystery Box 109

Glossary 113

References and Resources 115

Index 121

ABOUT THE AUTHORS

Eric C. Sheninger is the principal at New Milford High School in Bergen County, New Jersey. He is passionate about establishing and fostering learning environments that are student centered, collaborative, flexible, and capable of preparing all learners to succeed in the 21st century.

As an educational administrator, he firmly believes that effective communication, listening, support, shared decision making, and the integration of technology are essential elements for the transformation of school cultures. Eric has emerged as an innovative leader in the use of social media and web 2.0 technology as tools to engage students, improve communication with stakeholders, and help educators grow professionally. Eric is a 2012 National Association of Secondary School Principals Digital Principal Award recipient, Google Certified Teacher, Adobe Education Leader, ASCD 2011 Conference Scholar, blogger for the *Huffington Post*, and coauthor of *Communicating and Connecting With Social Media*, and he was named to the National School Boards Association "20 to Watch" list in 2010 for technology leadership. He now presents and speaks nationally to assist other school leaders in embracing and effectively utilizing technology. His blog, A Principal's Reflections, earned Best School Administrator Blog in 2011 from Edublogs.

Eric began his career in education as a science teacher at Watchung Hills Regional High School in Warren, New Jersey. He then transitioned into the field of educational administration as an athletic director and supervisor of physical education and health and as vice principal in the New Milford School District. During his administrative career, he has served as district affirmative action officer and is the current president of the New Milford Administrators' Association.

Eric earned a bachelor of science from Salisbury University, a bachelor of science from the University of Maryland Eastern Shore, and a master of education in educational administration from East Stroudsburg University.

To learn more about Eric's work, visit http://ericsheninger.com, or follow @NMHS_Principal on Twitter.

 **Keith Devereaux** is a biology teacher and STEM (science, technology, engineering, and mathematics) interdepartmental liaison for New Milford High School in Bergen County, New Jersey. Keith's goal is to incorporate relevant topics into the classroom in dynamic and engaging ways. Keith is fluent in many aspects of educational technology, and he uses technology as a way to drive home lesson goals.

Keith is also active in the school as a girls' volleyball coach, a freshman baseball coach, and an academic team coach. He is a member of the Intervention and Referral Services Team, Professional Development Committee and has served on various other school committees. Keith's professional development workshops focus on Google's web-based applications and how they can be integrated into science instruction.

To learn more about Keith's work, visit https://sites.google.com/site/mrdevereauxsscience classes, or follow @keith_devereaux on Twitter.

To book Eric or Keith for professional development, contact pd@solution-tree.com.

INTRODUCTION
LEADING CHANGE

Principals are pivotal to setting a positive tone and establishing a climate for sustainable increases in achievement. By *climate*, we mean how people feel about their school and the combination of stakeholders' shared values, attitudes, and beliefs. Stakeholders include students, teachers, administrators, parents, bus drivers, office personnel, custodians, cafeteria workers, and other people who play an instrumental role in the culture of the school. When you lead, you turn beliefs about science education into actions.

A principal who values a strong, comprehensive science program will establish the right climate by instilling pride in science teaching among his or her staff, modeling good science teaching and organizing his or her school in order to promote it, acknowledging success when it occurs, and protecting the values and beliefs that promote science teaching from the intrusion of state and federal mandates. To instill pride, a principal might say to his or her teachers, "We are on our way to becoming one of the premier schools in the state for science education." To model science teaching that works, a principal might ask someone to demonstrate a science lesson and host a conversation about it afterward. To acknowledge success, a principal could publicly recognize those teachers who entered the most students in the state science fair. Finally, to protect science teaching from intrusion, principals can jealously guard time allotted in teachers' schedules for that purpose.

Beginning the Process

At times, it can be quite intimidating to anticipate all that is needed to lead a school toward an improved focus on an interdisciplinary science program. To prepare the way, you can take four actions.

1. Prior to any substantial change initiative, assess your successes in curriculum, instruction, and student learning.

2. Engage your staff in a discussion on the many things they are doing already to foster inquiry-based thinking, incorporate STEM (science, technology, engineering, and mathematics), and promote hands-on learning.

3. Acknowledge the fear or discomfort learners may have with science. Determine through conversations what they know about experimental design or key scientific concepts.

4. Most importantly, assess stakeholders' desire to make science a shared value for the entire school community.

Holistic improvement is within reach once you determine that your staff members are ready and willing to invest their time and energy to work collaboratively in this endeavor. But real reform requires developing a vision, articulating a plan for change, and getting behind it. As the instructional and managerial leader of your school, you have the opportunity to influence many decisions that have a direct impact on science teaching. Specifically, you can do the following:

- Keep science interests and experiences in mind when hiring staff.
- Include current staff at some stage of the hiring process.
- Support your staff with the latest technology.
- Ensure that time is allocated in faculty meetings for learning more about science inquiry.
- Conduct formal and informal classroom visits during science instruction.
- Encourage thematic team planning centered on science concepts.
- Protect teacher setup time so that materials management is reasonable.
- Host student assemblies that honor student efforts in science.
- Provide relevant and meaningful professional development in K–8 science instruction.
- Distribute articles on science teaching prior to faculty meetings, as well as for summer reading.
- Brainstorm with teachers on a routine basis. Continuously ask them for their input and ideas on how to improve the overall science program.
- Include science items in staff newsletters, emails, and other correspondence.
- Share what teachers are doing through community newsletters and social media (blogs, Facebook, and Twitter, for example).
- Establish a science focus on the school's website.

Professional Development and Science Education

To develop a schoolwide passion for science, the entire school community must acknowledge the need to focus on science. In the 1950s, the launching of *Sputnik* sparked a national interest in science instruction. Since then, global competition and the emphasis on STEM as a pathway to greater societal sustainability have triggered a renewed sense of urgency in science education. As principals establish their school's needs and identify goals, they can lead their staff through a variety of initiatives, which we explore in this book, to transform the school into an innovative institution that focuses on quality science instruction.

Young learners have a natural affinity toward science, and science concepts and principles pervade all subjects. Educational leaders, principals, and teachers can invite scientists, engineers, and university professors to speak about career opportunities in the field to drive students' excitement. Students studying science have opportunities to practice problem solving and develop critical-thinking skills. Students use mathematics as they measure phenomena and quantify relationships. Science is the focus for resolving complex societal problems, such as environmental conservation and sustainability. Science involves history and language arts strategies. It provides a venue for creativity, innovation, exploration, and engagement with cutting-edge ideas that foster a love of learning. Asking questions, debating, analyzing data, defending ideas, and compromising—these are all part of scientific inquiry. Science is also fun and exciting and prepares students with 21st century skills that are essential for success in a constantly evolving global society. These essential elements of scientific thought and problem solving are found throughout all curricular areas.

About This Book

This second edition of *What Principals Need to Know About Teaching and Learning Science* addresses the essential elements of exemplary science programs while providing practical strategies for increasing science achievement in K–8. This book has been designed as a user-friendly resource to which principals can refer on a continuing basis to improve science instruction in collaboration with their staff. In addition to a comprehensive discussion of the important issues, it includes:

- Reproducible forms, checklists, and other materials to use in evaluating your school's science program and collaborating with all pertinent stakeholders (teachers, parents, and students)

- Lists of questions to consider as you develop a plan to improve instruction and increase science achievement

We've opened *What Principals Need to Know About Teaching and Learning Science* with recommendations on leading change to create a school climate that supports effective science instruction. In chapters 1 and 2, we discuss science instructional materials and science curricula. Chapter 3 offers a self-assessment survey of your science program. Data collected from this survey will assist in determining your school's strengths and weaknesses in regard to science instruction. In chapters 4 and 5, we consider inquiry-based learning and the assessment of science learning, as well as the design of science experiments. Finally, in chapter 6, we outline strategies for professional development to improve science teaching and outline guidelines for observing and evaluating science instruction. The appendices will provide you with valuable resources to refine your science programs and provide support to your teachers. Throughout each section of the book, the focus remains on the principal's role in coordinating the successful implementation of an effective science program.

The *What Principals Need to Know About* series is a curricular resource principals can refer to for concise, research-based information on the major subject areas in K–8 instruction. As the instructional leader in your building, you should be knowledgeable about effective pedagogical practices in each content area and be able to provide teachers with sound instructional feedback, suggestions, and support. We hope you will find this guide useful and will add value to it by recording your notes, observations, and additional Internet resources as you work to refine your school's science program.

ONE
SCIENTIFIC INQUIRY

Scientists share a set of attitudes and beliefs about the nature of our world and the means to investigate its secrets. For example, scientists presume that there are persistent patterns in the universe that can be identified through careful observation and systematic study. They also allow for change in scientific ideas and theories as new knowledge is discovered and new patterns are identified. Scientific knowledge is often described using the *best fit theory*, which states that one cohesive theory explains everything that is known about a topic and can be modified as new knowledge is obtained (Lederman & Lederman, 2004). For example, when new discoveries made it impossible to explain the movement of the planets with Earth in the center of the universe, Copernicus postulated that the planets circle the sun rather than the Earth.

According to Norman Lederman (1999), all students should know the following five tenets concerning the nature of science. Scientific knowledge is:

1. Tentative and therefore subject to change
2. Empirically based on or derived from observations of the natural world
3. Subjective and theory laden
4. Contingent on human inference, imagination, and creativity to develop explanations for occurrences
5. Socially and culturally embedded—a natural part of people's thought process

According to the National Science Teachers Association (NSTA, 2000a), "Science is characterized by the systematic gathering of information through various forms of direct and indirect observations and the testing of this information by methods including, but not limited to, experimentation." The NSTA (2007a) further states that "for science to be taught properly and effectively, labs must be an integral part of the science curriculum." In general, it is best for all learners to have multiple opportunities every week to engage in hands-on science activities in a lab situation.

Scientific Methods and Scientific Literacy

The *scientific method* is often referred to as a staple of effective science instruction. People once believed that scientists used just one method—a step-by-step process—for conducting research, and over the years, many students have had to memorize various lists of steps claiming to be *the* scientific method. But in fact, practicing scientists employ a broad spectrum of methods, and "it is only through engagement in the practices that students can recognize how such knowledge comes about and why some parts of scientific theory are more firmly established than others" (National Research Council [NRC], 2012, p. 43).

Figure 1.1 shows the scientific method in its simplified form.

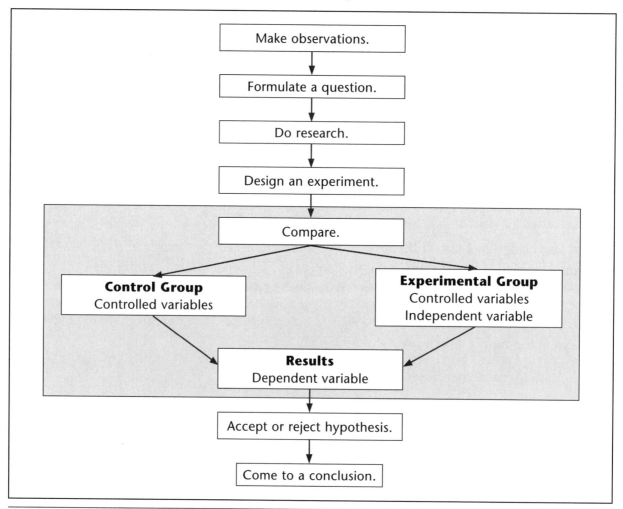

Figure 1.1: A simplified diagram of the process of scientific investigation.

Scientific inquiry is the means by which one attains the deeper understanding of science that we call science literacy. Scientific inquiry allows students to investigate problems, utilizing their knowledge of the scientific method and designing their own experiments and questions to learn about scientific topics. It puts the learner in the shoes of the scientist. According to the NRC (1996), "Lifelong scientific literacy begins with attitudes and values established in the earliest years" (p. 18). At the heart of scientific literacy are the habits of making observations, asking questions, exploring natural phenomena, conducting experiments, finding patterns in data, seeking knowledge, and solving problems. Methods of teaching using inquiry foster scientific curiosity in children.

A central strategy for inquiry is to start with science questions that students generate from their own experiences. In this way, science becomes an active process in which students engage in *hands-on* investigations as well as *minds-on* analyses of observations. Hands-on learning coupled with active inquiry is time consuming and resource intensive, yet it is one of the highest priorities of the greater science education community.

An Example of Scientific Investigation: What Makes Yeast Rise?

A science teacher conducts an experiment to show his classes that yeast will produce gas when mixed with certain solutions but not others. The teacher illustrates this by mixing yeast with apple juice in one flask and with water in another. The teacher then puts a balloon over both flasks, and students watch what happens to each balloon throughout the course of the day.

They notice that the balloon over the apple juice begins to inflate, while the balloon over the water does not. The teacher does this setup with two different classes, placing one class's flasks on a desk in the back of the room and the other set on the windowsill. By the end of the day, the balloons covering the flasks on the windowsill are significantly more inflated than the ones in the back of the room. This arouses the curiosity of the students, and a flurry of questions follow.

Student 1: Why is the one by the window bigger?

Teacher: Why do you think?

Student 1: Because it is in the sun?

Teacher: That's possible; are there any other thoughts?

Student 2: Maybe it got hotter by the window, and the higher temperature made the yeast eat the sugar faster.

Teacher: How does eating sugar make the balloon get bigger?

Student 3: The byproduct of the yeast eating the sugar is carbon dioxide. The more sugar the yeast eat, the more carbon dioxide they produce.

Teacher: Good. Those are both great thoughts. How could you test them? I would like everyone to select one of those two hypotheses and design a scientific experiment to test if either or both of those factors affected the results of my demonstration.

The scientific method is already underway in this scenario. Referring back to the sequence in figure 1.1 (page 6), we now have an observation, a question, and a hypothesis.

- **Observation:** The apple juice and yeast flask on the windowsill inflated the balloon more quickly.
- **Question:** Why did the apple juice and yeast flask inflate the balloon more quickly?
- **Student 2's hypothesis:** Sugar consumption by yeast increases with the temperature of the environment, thus producing more carbon dioxide.

Student 2 designs the following *controlled experiment.*

Fill three flasks with 30 mL of apple juice and one packet of baker's yeast. Wrap each flask in aluminum foil so that light cannot get into the flask. Place one flask in the refrigerator (4 °C), one flask in room temperature (~23 °C), and one in a hot-water bath (40 °C).

To ensure proper experimental design, the teacher has the students list their variables on a worksheet to help them lay out their procedure and experiment. Student 2 labels the following as his variables.

- **Independent variable:** Temperature of the three environments
- **Dependent variable:** Rate of inflation of the balloons
- **Controlled variables:** Volume of apple juice, quantity of yeast, type of juice, type of yeast, foil wrapped around flasks to block light

Table 1.1 shows Student 2's findings after one day.

Table 1.1: Diameter of Balloons as a Means of Measuring Gas Production of Yeast

Time	4 °C Flask	23 °C Flask	40 °C Flask
9:00 a.m.	0 cm	0 cm	0 cm
10:00 a.m.	0 cm	6 cm	12 cm
11:00 a.m.	4 cm	9 cm	18 cm
12:00 p.m.	5 cm	14 cm	24 cm
1:00 p.m.	5 cm	20 cm	31 cm

Student 2 is able to show that the balloon in the warmest environment inflates at a faster rate than the other two balloons and is thus able to accept the hypothesis that yeast will increase its sugar consumption as the temperature of the environment increases.

The Nature of Science

Science helps satisfy natural curiosity. The following premises are important to understanding the nature of science:

- Scientific knowledge is simultaneously reliable and tentative. Having confidence in scientific knowledge is reasonable, realizing that such knowledge may be abandoned or modified in light of new evidence or reconceptualization of prior evidence and knowledge.

> - Although no single universal step-by-step scientific method captures the complexity of doing science, a number of shared values and perspectives characterize a scientific approach to understanding nature. Among these is a demand for naturalistic explanations that empirical evidence supports and are, at least in principle, testable against the natural world. Other shared elements include observations, rational argument, inference, skepticism, peer review, and replicability of work.
> - Creativity is a vital yet personal ingredient in the production of scientific knowledge.
> - Science by definition is limited to naturalistic methods and explanations and as such is precluded from using supernatural elements in the production of scientific knowledge.
> - A primary goal of science is the formation of theories and laws, which include terms with very specific meanings.
> - People worldwide make scientific contributions.
> - The existing state of scientific knowledge, the social and cultural context of the researcher, and the observer's experiences and expectations influence scientific questions, observations, and conclusions.
> - The history of science reveals both evolutionary and revolutionary changes. New evidence and interpretation replace or supplement old ideas.
> - While science and technology do impact each other, basic scientific research is not directly concerned with practical outcomes but rather with gaining an understanding of the natural world for its own sake.
>
> *Source: NSTA, 2000a.*

A Global Consensus

For the 2011 *Trends in International Mathematics and Science Study* (TIMSS), more than sixty nations agreed to foster in students a general knowledge of scientific inquiry and the nature of science. The emphasis was on inquiry, with students expected to demonstrate their knowledge of the tools and methods necessary to do science, apply knowledge in order to engage in scientific investigations, and use scientific understanding to propose explanations based on evidence (Mullis et al., 2011). Students were asked to demonstrate this by:

- Formulating questions and hypotheses
- Designing investigations
- Collecting and representing data
- Analyzing and interpreting data
- Drawing conclusions and developing explanations

Guiding Principles and Goals for K–8 Science Programs

According to the NRC (2012), students who are immersed in an effective science program should gain sufficient knowledge of the practices, crosscutting scientific concepts and core ideas of science and engineering to enable them to engage in public discussions on science-related issues; be critical consumers of scientific information related to their everyday experience; and continue to learn about science throughout their lives. Schools can contribute to helping students develop these critical skills by providing science education that is based on four very simple but key principles (Barnett, Yamagata-Lynch, Keating, Barab, & Hay, 2005; NRC, 2007).

1. Children are born investigators. Research reveals that children entering kindergarten have surprisingly sophisticated ways of thinking about the world, based in part on their direct experiences with the physical environment (NRC, 2012).

2. Science is a natural endeavor that each of us uses every day. We routinely question what we see and then try to figure out explanations for our observations. These are major components of the scientific method.

3. The use of multimedia and modeling tools, especially those utilizing 3-D technology, greatly aids in the mastery and learning of science concepts by creating engaging opportunities for learners to create, manipulate, and interact with their own constructions, which in turn support them in developing understandings through their firsthand experience.

4. Learning science is its own reward. Discovering new information about the world around us or figuring out how something works is thrilling as well as empowering.

These principles set a context for the goals of student learning in the classroom and the importance of science literacy for responsible decision making. In addition to these four principles, all science instruction should be based on four common goals. According to the NRC (1996), students should have the opportunity to:

1. Experience the richness and excitement that come with knowledge and understanding of the natural world

2. Apply scientific processes and principles in order to make decisions

3. Engage in intelligent public discussion and debate about matters pertaining to science and technology

4. Develop a capacity for economic productivity during their worklife through the use of the knowledge, understanding, and skills associated with being a scientifically literate person

The NRC's (1996) recommendations also include shifting the emphasis in science teaching in specific ways that promote inquiry. See table 2.1.

Table 2.1: Shifting the Emphasis in Science Education to Promote Inquiry

Less Emphasis On	More Emphasis On
Planning activities that demonstrate and verify science content	Planning activities that investigate and analyze science questions
Confining investigations to a single class period	Investigating over extended periods of time
Processing skills out of context	Processing skills in context

Less Emphasis On	More Emphasis On
Emphasizing individual process skills, such as observation or inference	Using multiple process skills—manipulative, cognitive, and procedural
Arriving at an answer	Using evidence and strategies for developing or revising an explanation
Exploring and experimenting	Debating and explaining results
Providing answers to questions about science content	Communicating science explanations
Having individual and groups of students analyze and synthesize data without defending a conclusion	Having groups of students analyze and synthesize data after defending conclusions
Doing minimal investigations in order to leave time to cover the curriculum	Doing more investigations in order to develop understanding, ability, values of inquiry, and knowledge of science content
Concluding inquiries with the result of the experiment	Applying the results of experiments to scientific arguments and explanations
Managing materials and equipment	Managing ideas and information
Privately communicating student ideas and conclusions to the teacher	Publicly communicating student ideas and work to classmates

Source: Adapted from NRC, 1996.

Origins of the Science Reform Movement

The science reform movement started in 1985, when the American Association for the Advancement of Science (AAAS) led an investigation to identify what every high school graduate should know and be able to do in science. Its (1989) report, *Science for All Americans*, eventually led to the research-based science education reform documents we have been examining here. Discussions began heating up in 2012 about how to update the national standards. NRC (2012) released a conceptual framework for the new National Science Education Standards. It represents a first step in the process to revise the standards NRC established in 1996. The following resources detail science education standards:

- *Benchmarks for Science Literacy* (AAAS, 1993)
- *National Science Education Standards* (NRC, 1996)
- *Framework for K–12 Science Education* (NRC, 2012)

Development of National Standards

Benchmarks for Science Literacy (AAAS, 1993) and the *National Science Education Standards* (NRC, 1996) were key steps in establishing a cohesive research base to guide science teaching. *Benchmarks for Science Literacy* specifies the core content students should learn at each grade level. The *National Science Education Standards* (NRC, 1996) is a parallel and compatible document that also specifies core content knowledge at specified grade levels. (According to AAAS [1997], there is a 90 percent overlap in the science content recommendations of these two documents.)

These consensus documents from the science and education communities discuss what students should know and be able to do in science as well as how science should be taught. NRC (2000) notes that student learning and effective science instruction inform the development of these standards and will continue to influence the development of new ones. NRC (2000) notes that in regard to science, students should:

- Understand that it goes well beyond the memorization of facts
- Be able to formulate new knowledge by modifying and refining current scientific concepts and by adding new ones to what they already know
- Be aware that the learning process is facilitated by the social and cultural process of interacting with others
- Be able to take control of their own learning
- Possess the ability to apply knowledge to authentic situations—that is, to effect the transfer of learning as a result of conceptual understanding

The professionalization of science teaching requires that all decisions concerning science education, including policies, curriculum, instruction, assessment, and evaluation, be research based (NSTA, 2010). Research provides the best pedagogical techniques to enhance student learning and improve achievement in the sciences. If current research on best practices is not consistently incorporated, achieving and sustaining an effective science program will be compromised. Pedagogy and research should not be separate endeavors. Chapter 6 (page 67) will explore teachers' classroom research as a form of teacher professional development. The NRC recommends teachers do the following four actions to best teach science (Donovan & Bransford, 2005):

1. Address initial understandings and preconceptions students have about topics
2. Organize knowledge around the core concept
3. Support metacognition and student self-regulation through the use of instructional strategies that allow students to take control of their own learning
4. Develop and routinely use cooperative learning activities

STEM Promotion

More and more initiatives are being created to incorporate STEM into daily instruction across the United States. Additionally, school leaders must analyze equity issues to establish substantial reform that will allow all students to flourish (NRC, 2012; NSTA, 2003). NRC (2012) suggests the following initiatives to promote STEM:

- Ensuring science and engineering learning for all to promote scientific literacy and knowledge of 21st century occupations
- Creating equal opportunity for all socioeconomic groups to learn science

- Using inclusive instruction that encompasses a variety of teaching strategies and approaches that build on students' interests and backgrounds to increase engagement
- Approaching science learning as a cultural accomplishment; viewing the learning of science as important as the learning of math and language arts
- Relating scientific discourses to youth discourses, in which students have formal conversations in written and oral form on science concepts, processes, and phenomena
- Building on prior interest and identity
- Valuing multiple modes of expression

Support for reform is extensive in the science education community. The NSTA (1998) asserts that:

- Teachers, regardless of grade level, should promote inquiry-based instruction and provide classroom environments and experiences that facilitate students' learning of science
- Professional development activities should involve teachers in the learning of science and pedagogy through inquiry, and integrate knowledge of science, learning, and pedagogy
- Teachers should continually assess both their own teaching and student learning
- Assessment practices should be varied and focus on both achievement and opportunity to learn, be consistent with the decisions they are designed to inform, and result in sound and fair decisions and inferences
- Subject matter stress should be on in-depth understandings of unifying concepts, principles, and themes, with less emphasis placed upon lower-level skills, such as the memorization of numerous facts
- Inquiry should be viewed as an instructional outcome (knowing and doing) for students to achieve in addition to its use as a pedagogical approach
- Science programs should provide equitable opportunities for all students and should be developmentally appropriate, interesting, and relevant to students; inquiry-oriented; and coordinated with other subject matter and curricula
- Science programs should be viewed as an integral part of a larger educational system that should have policies that are consistent with, and support, all standards areas and are coordinated across all relevant agencies, institutions, and organizations

The Common Core State Standards movement has taken the national stage. As of this publication, forty-five U.S. states have adopted the standards. They provide a clear understanding of what students are expected to learn, so teachers and parents are prepared to assist them.

The standards are designed to be robust and relevant to the real world, reflecting the knowledge and skills that our students need for success in college and careers (National Governors Association Center for Best Practices & Council of Chief State School Officers, 2012). Visit www.corestandards.org/the-standards for the specific reading and writing literacy standards for science.

The National Science Education Standards (NRC, 1996) provide a foundation for reform in science teaching, professional development, assessment, science content, school programs, and school systems. These standards provide a guide for state standards and curriculum development. There are no mandates to follow. Revised standards will greatly assist school leaders and teachers in continuing this effort. Additionally, the Next Generation Science Standards, based on the *Framework for K–12 Science Education* (NRC, 2012), will provide a statewide set of science content expectations for college and career readiness. These standards are slated for release in late 2012 or early 2013. Visit www.nextgenscience.org for more information.

National Science Teachers Association

The NSTA is an organization of more than sixty thousand science teachers and others dedicated to science education. The reform effort is supported through its Science Matters program, as well as regional and national conferences, its publications, and its website. In Science Matters, NSTA plans to increase awareness and develop a sense of urgency among U.S. schools and communities as to the importance of science literacy and education.

Each year, NSTA sponsors one national conference and a series of regional conferences for science teachers that thousands of teachers attend. NSTA publications include a fifty-two-page newspaper, *NSTA Reports*, and four peer-reviewed professional journals, *Science and Children* (elementary school), *Science Scope* (middle school), *The Science Teacher* (secondary school), and the *Journal of College Science Teaching* (college). The NSTA website (www.nsta.org) provides an extensive source of science resources at all grade levels for teachers, administrators, and parents.

Source: NSTA, 2002.

Summary

Inquiry is an integral component of science learning. Allowing learners to use their own ideas and questions to fuel conceptual learning is an important aspect of learning science on which teachers should focus. Aiding your staff in fostering this perspective is an important step in the process of establishing an effective science program. Allow your teachers to search for professional growth opportunities that will encourage inquiry in the classroom. If you are able to, attend a seminar on inquiry-based teaching and learning strategies, as this will allow you to be a resource to your staff. Inquiry, when used effectively, can greatly enhance the environment of a science classroom while promoting critical thought and problem-solving skill sets.

TWO
SCIENCE CURRICULA

Each U.S. state is responsible for determining the content that public school students are required to know. Some states' standards are very specific and list the science concepts required at each grade level K–12. Other states follow the approach of the national science standards (NRC, 1996) and specify what students should know by the time they complete a certain group of grade levels. In elementary public school classrooms across the United States, content in life science, earth science, and physical science is usually taught in each grade level. Local education authorities (LEAs) usually decide how these science standards or objectives are taught. In contrast to the traditional school science topics of life science, earth science, and physical science, the U.S. National Science Education Standards (NRC, 1996) provide an expanded perspective of what students should know, understand, and be able to do in the natural sciences over the course of K–12 education (NRC, 1996). They are organized into eight categories:

1. Unifying concepts and processes in science
2. Science as inquiry
3. Physical science
4. Life science
5. Earth and space science
6. Science and technology
7. Science in personal and social perspective
8. History and nature of science (NRC, 1996, p. 6)

In 2012, the NRC introduced a framework for new science standards with an emphasis on the traditional topics (life science, earth and space science, and physical science) as well as engineering, technology, and application of science. Within this framework, the NRC (2012) considers eight practices as essential elements of a K–12 science and engineering curriculum:

1. Asking questions (for science) and defining problems (for engineering)
2. Developing and using models
3. Planning and carrying out investigations
4. Analyzing and interpreting data
5. Using mathematics, information and computer technology, and computational thinking
6. Constructing explanations (for science) and designing solutions (for engineering)
7. Engaging in argument from evidence
8. Obtaining, evaluating, and communicating information (pp. 46–47)

Your School's Science Content

The scope and quality of K–8 science programs vary greatly. At one end of the spectrum are programs that science curriculum supervisors develop in collaboration with teachers. These documents possess all the required standards, benchmarks, and indicators established for each grade level. They usually have complementary teacher guides with detailed unit plans and lessons. They often list approved print materials, science equipment, manipulatives, Internet resources, and multimedia materials. Additionally, these documents may also contain pedagogical techniques, differentiated assessment strategies, evaluation activities, and information on how to adapt lessons for students with special needs.

At the other end of the spectrum are school systems that do not have science curriculum supervisors and may use state science standards and benchmarks as their science program without providing a framework for teachers to discuss and truly understand them. Some school districts will simply adopt a publisher's textbook and use that as a basis for teaching elementary science. In either case, the teacher makes ultimate decisions about what science is actually taught in the elementary classroom.

As the instructional leader, the principal must (1) understand the science curriculum, (2) determine when content is taught, and (3) ensure that instruction follows the established program.

Understand the Science Curriculum

The first step is to familiarize yourself with the science content required for each grade level. You may be surprised to see that the third-grade dinosaur unit is a favorite of the teachers but is not a required component at all in the third-grade science curriculum. You may also note that the textbook you are using in fifth grade has no content on the classification of organisms, yet this topic is one of the fifth-grade benchmarks. Before purchasing textbooks, teachers and administrators should collaboratively review the books and compare their contents to your school district's curriculum, as well as to the state and national standards. This is a great opportunity for you as the school leader to collaboratively confer with your teachers and make the right decision together for learners.

Many states have standardized science tests that cover the content outlined in their respective core curriculum content standards. It is a sound practice to routinely analyze your elementary science program in order to ensure that it is aligned with the state standards. Doing so will allow you and your teachers to best determine if all students are being provided the necessary content and hands-on experiences to ensure success on standardized tests.

Determine When Content Is Taught

The next step is to determine *when* required content should be taught. If your school system does not provide a quarterly management plan for covering the required science concepts, then facilitate the development of an outline or bulleted list of concepts to be taught in each quarter. This information can be put into a chart or Google Doc and shared with all teachers responsible for science instruction in order to help budget effectively for materials, as these will be in high demand during particular time periods. A science curriculum chart organized by grade level and quarter has a number of other useful functions. It allows you to check whether science topics other than the required material are being taught, it can serve as a ready reference to disseminate information to parents, and it will be useful during parent conferences, open houses, and orientation events, and when planning for a science fair.

Ensure That Instruction Follows the Established Program

If you have followed steps one and two, you should have a good idea of what is being taught and a quarterly schedule of when the material should be covered. The difficult part is making sure it *is* taught. At the elementary level, there are usually three factors that influence whether science is being taught, and taught appropriately. They are:

1. Scheduling the time to teach science

2. Designing and implementing pertinent professional development opportunities for teachers so they have the knowledge base and skills to teach science

3. Providing the teachers with the materials and other support structures they need to teach science

Scheduling Time

Science teaching in elementary schools often falls by the wayside—unlike language arts and mathematics, which are driven by the pressure of standardized tests. In fact, many schools spend three or less hours per week teaching science. This is not nearly enough time to adequately teach the content and to allow students to practice, internalize, and master the concepts in order to demonstrate learning and comprehension.

With math and language arts being so scrutinized at the elementary and middle school levels, it is understandable that many schools put science on the back burner. However, scientific thinking needs to be established early on—before high school—in order for students to succeed later and acquire 21st century skills. Too often, students are merely given science content without a chance to actually partake in scientific inquiry. These cognitive abilities need to be developed at the elementary levels.

Meet with the grade-level teams and establish an effective plan for integrating science into instruction each day. For instance, on some days, it may be a short fifteen-minute review or a warm-up activity to pique student interest in an upcoming unit. Science can be integrated into any other area via interdisciplinary lessons; however, there should be at least two longer blocks of time each week to critically investigate a science topic in depth or engage in a hands-on, inquiry-based learning activity. As the instructional leader, you need to work creatively with grade-level teams to infuse time in the complicated school schedule to teach science.

Finding Ways to Support Staff

It is essential that science teachers be provided professional development opportunities both in and out of the district. In order to adjust to changing curricula and state standards, quality instruction in the sciences relies on the ability of school leaders to provide access to adequate workshops, trainings, webinars, and conferences. This becomes crucial as more schools begin to integrate STEM into the science curriculum. Although this might cost money, it is imperative that teachers have the knowledge, pedagogical techniques, and skills to maximize conceptual understanding and student learning. A powerful and cost-effective form of professional development would be to form teacher teams. This is discussed in detail in chapter 6 (page 67).

Providing Materials and Other Support Structures

Teaching science tends to be more expensive than other curricular areas because of lab supplies, classroom design, field trips, chemicals, specialized equipment, and simulation software. If the expectations are to deliver high-quality instruction, effectively integrate technology, and promote inquiry-based learning, proper funds need to be allocated to purchase materials. The creation of new courses and curricula will surely drive expenditures, especially in the area of STEM. During this exciting process, principals should empower their teachers by allowing them to have a great deal of input into what items will be purchased to support the science program. In addition to resources, other essential support structures include release time for professional development, field trips, and team- and grade-level meetings and the development of a schedule that supports meaningful science instruction.

Curricular Alignment

Research shows that curricular alignment of the intended curriculum (the science that society intends for students to learn), the implemented curriculum (what is actually taught), and the attained curriculum (what students have learned) leads to systemic increases in school performance (Mullis et al., 2011; Squires, 2009). Newmann, Smith, Allensworth, and Bryk (2001) suggest three major conditions for curricular coherence:

1. A common instructional framework that guides curriculum, instruction, assessment, and learning climate, combining specific expectations for student learning with specific strategies and materials to guide teaching assessment

2. Staff working conditions that support implementation of the framework

3. Resources—materials, time, and staff assignments—to advance the school's common instructional framework and improvement efforts

---

Components of Coherent K–12 Science Education Curriculum Programs

Goals should:
- Clearly specify the target audience
- Communicate broad outcomes and values
- Provide guidance
- Describe student outcomes, not system outcomes
- Be widely accepted
- Not be modified frequently

Content standards should:
- Cover fundamental content
- Be scientifically accurate
- Be written in understandable vocabulary

Curriculum framework should:
- Be assigned to grade levels based on what students are capable of learning
- Indicate development of processes, skills, and abilities over several years
- Clearly indicate which standards are prerequisites for others
- Be appropriately balanced and concentrated
- Contain concepts that are grouped to form the basis of units or courses, with logical connections shown both within a grouping and across grades
- Account for all standards

Instructional materials should:
- Be scientifically accurate, consistent with the outcomes in standards, and targeted at the level called for in the framework
- Support research that makes it possible for students to attain specific outcomes
- Align with the content and level of skill expected in the standards
- Accompany evidence from field trials showing that students can learn the specified content and skills if the materials are used as intended

Source: Adapted from NRC, 1999.

Why does instructional coherence promote student achievement? Newmann et al. (2001) explain:

> Compared to disconnected short-term experiences, integrated experiences, sustained long enough for successful completion, provide greater clarity about what is required for mastery, and how prior knowledge can be applied to future questions. Students learning to read, for example, are more likely to gain basic skills, and the confidence to tackle more challenging tasks, in settings where all of their teachers assist their reading in a consistent manner. (p. 15)

The following questions can assist you in determining how well curriculum and instruction are aligned in your school:

- Is there an agreed-on written set of standards that outlines what is to be taught?
- Do the teachers teach the intended curriculum?
- Are the textbooks or other resource materials aligned with the written standards?
- How often do teachers depend on a textbook to tell them the content to teach?
- How often do teachers teach subjects aligned with their own interest even if they are not in the standards?
- How often has an outside norm-referenced test been the single indicator of science achievement?

When the intended curriculum is well planned, aligned to the appropriate standards, and implemented, the intended outcomes will assist students in acquiring basic skills they need to be successful in all aspects of life, not just science.

Cognitive Domains

Effective science curricular materials authentically engage students in observing, analyzing, interpreting, and evaluating science information at multiple cognitive levels. Cognitive domains in science span all relevant subcontent areas and fall into three major categories: (1) factual knowledge, (2) conceptual understanding, and (3) reasoning and analysis (Mullis et al., 2011). Mullis et al. (2011) note that the following specific teaching practices support students' cognitive development in each domain:

1. **Factual knowledge:**
    - Recall and recognize
    - Define
    - Describe
    - Illustrate with examples
    - Demonstrate knowledge of scientific instruments

2. **Conceptual understanding:**
   - Compare, contrast, and classify
   - Use models
   - Relate
   - Interpret information
   - Find solutions
   - Explain
3. **Reasoning and analysis:**
   - Analyze
   - Integrate and synthesize
   - Hypothesize or predict
   - Design or plan investigations
   - Draw conclusions
   - Generalize
   - Evaluate
   - Justify

A Further Look at Curricular Materials and Activities

The adoption of new science materials in your school should serve as a catalyst to update the science program and place a greater emphasis on STEM instruction. Establishing a science curriculum-adoption committee, obtaining quality materials to evaluate, and creating a process that includes criteria to review materials fairly are crucial steps to ensure that all teachers and administrators participate and engage in this collaborative process. To engage all learners, adopt curricular materials that base science instruction on critical and timely problems (Jacobs, 2010).

In order to form a curriculum-adoption committee, you will need to determine who the stakeholders are in this collaborative decision-making process. The committee should include a balance of teachers, school personnel, parents, and community members. Although the input from all groups is beneficial, the feedback that you receive from teachers is most valuable, as teachers are the only ones who have direct knowledge of using curricular materials with students. To ensure students a smooth science transition from grade to grade, schools should place at least one teacher from each grade level on this committee.

As we mentioned previously, obtaining quality materials to review is essential. The year prior to adopting any materials, try to send representatives to the NSTA national conference or a comparable state conference, which many states hold annually. Many textbook- and kit-based companies will have displays in the exhibit area, with knowledgeable personnel on hand. Attending one of these conferences can save hours of work locating good materials and arranging to have them sent to your school to preview. As an incentive, many companies give sample materials away for free (so bring a bag for all of your freebies!). In addition to going to conferences, check online for award-winning curricular materials. The U.S. Department of Education routinely evaluates curricular materials and is a great place to start.

Establish a process and criteria for collectively reviewing curricular materials with the staff, as this can be useful in all areas, not just science. In general, you want accurate, concept-based science material that is unbiased and appropriate for all students. Include materials that (Ogan-Bekiroglu, 2007):

- Provide a sense of purpose
- Take account of student ideas
- Engage students with relevant phenomena
- Develop and use scientific ideas
- Promote student thinking about phenomena, experiences, and knowledge
- Assess progress
- Enhance the science learning environment

In most curriculum packages, there is an abundance of superb support materials, including teacher editions, online versions of the textbook, websites (simulations, interactives, virtual manipulatives, videos, tutorials, and so on), test banks, assessment activities, DVDs, CDs for teachers that allow for customizing materials (for example, lab experiments, printouts, and assessments), and CDs with simulations for students.

Grade-level teams should guide the review process, as they are the guiding influence for making curricular decisions. Teachers should review potential new materials independently before discussing them as a team. After the grade-level teams have reviewed and recommended materials, the materials should be examined across grade levels. Vertical articulation among the grades is important and will lead to some necessary changes in grade-level team recommendations. The key here is to conduct thorough research in house prior to adopting any new curricular materials. Avoid solicitation by companies that offer special incentives to purchase their products, as this is a common pitfall leading to regretful purchases. The reproducible "Evaluating Science Curricular Materials" (page 74 and online at **go.solution-tree .com/leadership**) will assist you in effectively evaluating curricular materials being considered for purchase.

Using Textbooks Appropriately

Textbooks can be used as an effective part of science instruction, but they should not form the core of instruction, especially in the early grades of elementary school. This is because textbooks do not always support effective inquiry learning unless they come with hands-on materials or your staff develop or supplement these activities. Foley and McPhee (2008) find that students in science classes in which teachers routinely use hands-on learning activities have a better understanding of the nature of science and are generally more favorable to it than students in textbook classes.

Textbooks are best used for student reference, with regard to scientific ideas and concepts or to consult when students are looking for confirmation of experimental results. Steven Anderson, district instructional technologist for the Winston-Salem/Forsyth County Schools in North Carolina, sees FlexBooks or OpenTexts as more appropriate reference books:

> These are books that are freely available online that allow schools or districts to customize the content and resources in them, as necessary. . . . Students and teachers no longer have to wait for the next edition to get fresh content in their classrooms. Additionally they allow for the creation of student-generated content, which is something we do not see in traditional textbooks. (S. Anderson, personal communication, June 30, 2011)

CK–12 Foundation has created some excellent FlexBooks covering the sciences (www.ck12.org/flexbook).

Some textbook-based middle school curricular materials have done a fantastic job addressing scientific concepts and principles. The U.S. Department of Education has rated Foundational Approaches in Science Teaching (FAST) as an exemplary science program, and it is highly coveted by science teachers (Bayer Corporation, 2010). FAST uses a sequence of three inquiry science courses for middle school. The three courses are the following.

FAST 1: The local environment

FAST 2: Matter and energy in the biosphere

FAST 3: Change over time

The content in each course is organized into three strands—physical science, ecology, and relational study. (Relational study focuses on the inter-relationship between the science disciplines and on science and society interactions.)

Using Science Kits

A science kit comprises print materials needed to implement a coherent unit of science study. Your staff can purchase or develop science kits. Kit-based materials are an effective method for providing materials that lead to effective inquiry-based and hands-on science instruction. Consider the following science kits.

- Full Option Science System (FOSS; www.fossweb.com) is a kit-based elementary school science program that the Lawrence Hall of Science in California developed. Its goal is to provide meaningful science education for all students in diverse classrooms. FOSS incorporates methodologies such as hands-on inquiry and interdisciplinary projects with contemporary methodologies, such as collaborative learning groups and multisensory observation. The FOSS programs are also fun for the kids to use and are teacher friendly.

- Science and Technology for Children™ (STC) and Science and Technology Concepts for Middle Schools (STC/MS) are inquiry-based, hands-on science programs for K–8 students (www.carolinacurriculum.com/STC) that the National Science Resources Center at the Smithsonian Institution in Washington, DC, developed. The STC kit has four modules per grade level and STC/MS has eight modules per grade level, each based on a four-stage learning cycle and designed to develop critical-thinking and problem-solving skills. These are great resources to teachers, as each includes balanced content in the life, earth, and physical sciences, as well as technology.

- Insights (http://cse.edc.org/curriculum/insightsElem) is a hands-on, inquiry-based elementary school science curriculum that the Education Development Center in Massachusetts developed for grades K–6. Its seventeen modules reflect a balance of life, physical, and earth sciences. They are structured to deliver hands-on, age-appropriate experiences that are directly relevant to each student.

- Great Explorations in Math and Science (GEMS) is an interdisciplinary curriculum program for students from preschool through eighth grade that the Lawrence Hall of Science at the University of California, Berkeley, developed (http://lhsgems.org). GEMS provides extended explorations of core topics including embedded assessments and enrichment opportunities, as well as STEM and literacy connections.

- Activities Integrating Mathematics and Science (AIMS; www.aimsedu.org) is a collection of activity books with integrated science and mathematics activities for grades K–9, manipulatives, and professional development opportunities. The premise behind AIMS materials is to develop conceptual understanding of science and math through hands-on activities that engage the learner.

Using Trade Books

Science trade books are a valuable resource that can augment the science curriculum. Since 1973, the NSTA and the Children's Book Council have jointly released an annual list of outstanding science trade books for students in grades K–12. The books on this list represent the best science trade books published in a particular year. Recommended reading levels and connections to the National Science Education Standards are included in each annotation. Visit www.nsta.org/publications/ostb to view the lists. Visit **go.solution-tree.com/leadership** to access the links mentioned in this book.

Creating Laboratory Activities

Laboratory activities provide an authentic opportunity for students to develop, refine, and enhance their process, as well as their analytical, communication, and conceptualization skills. A school laboratory investigation (also referred to as a *lab*) is defined as an experience in the laboratory, classroom, or field that provides students with opportunities to interact directly with natural phenomena or with data others collect using tools, materials, data-collection techniques, and models (NRC, 2006). When students practice process skills in all the cognitive domains, they construct their own understanding by discovering meaningful information and relationships. Often, this learning occurs through inquiry-driven student investigations of scientific principles. It is imperative that these investigations take place in a safe environment with proper precautions. The following practices are recommended for laboratory investigations.

- At the elementary level, students should have continuous opportunities to explore familiar phenomena and materials. At developmentally appropriate levels, they should investigate appropriate questions, analyze the results of lab investigations, debate what the evidence means, construct an understanding of science concepts, and apply these concepts to the world around them (NSTA, 2007a).

- In the middle and high school classroom, laboratory investigations should help all students develop a growing understanding of the complexity and ambiguity of empirical work, as well as the skills to calibrate and troubleshoot equipment used to make observations. Learners should understand measurement error and have the skills to aggregate, interpret, and present the resulting data (NRC, 2006).

Remember that even if your school does not have a science laboratory, teachers can still conduct science labs. Many activities do not require a physical laboratory to be completed. Teachers can often complete laboratory activities in a standard classroom with some slight creative modifications (and a quick Internet search). However, student safety cannot be compromised. Some labs cannot be conducted safely within a standard classroom, and you and your teachers need to be aware of this. Consult with teachers to determine if a lab-approval process should be implemented in your school in order to ensure the collaborative review of any questionable lab practices taking place during science instruction.

Designing Effective Science Experiments

A primary reason students have difficulty designing their own experiments is the existence of multiple variables. In order for an experiment to prove relationships, variables need to be controlled so that only one variable is being purposefully changed and only one variable is being measured. All other variables should be held constant. (Refer back to page 7 for a sample experiment on what makes yeast rise using constants and variables.)

Using the term *fair test* seems to help children understand the overall process of controlling the experimental design of a lab experiment. In conducting fair tests, students identify relevant variables, form hypotheses, conduct controlled experiments, interpret data, and draw conclusions. Having students analyze examples of well-designed experiments and identify the flaws in poorly designed experiments is a good way to get them thinking about proper experimental design before they actually design an experiment.

Hypotheses do not have to be written as "if, then" statements, but this is a helpful way to get students started. In the experimental design diagram, *if* is always followed by the independent variable, and *then* is followed by the dependent variable. The other two blanks in the "if, then" statement indicate how the variable will change. Choosing among *increase*, *decrease*, or *remain the same* options usually specifies the change. In our yeast experiment on page 7, for example, the hypothesis is, "If the temperature of the environment increases, then the sugar consumption by yeast will increase." The independent variable following *if* is the temperature, and the dependent variable following *then* is the sugar consumption.

Titles for experiments can be written as essential questions or as statements showing the relationship between the independent and dependent variable. For example, the student's yeast experiment in chapter 1 could appropriately be titled "The Effect of Temperature on Sugar Consumption in Yeast."

Although teachers are responsible for making experiments simple and clear, many are unsure of how to do so. Cothron, Giese, and Rezba's (2000) experimental design process in *Students and Research* is a simple and straightforward method of organizing scientifically accurate laboratory experiments.

A blank "Experimental Design Diagram," based on the work of Cothron et al. (2000), can be found on page 76 (and online at **go.solution-tree.com/leadership**). Teachers find the experimental design diagram easy to use and helpful in guiding student thinking as students plan experiments. Later, using the blank diagrams, students can create and plan their own experiments. When students fill out an experimental design diagram, they often identify and fix their own errors. In addition, because the diagram is easy to read, teachers can quickly identify students who are having trouble. In time, students can attempt the design process on their own without this support, using *outside-the-box* thinking to approach problems in new and innovative ways.

Identifying Patterns in Data

Scientists always look for patterns when they collect data. Finding a pattern is the first step in creating explanations. In order to facilitate this process, scientists use data tables or graphs to organize data. Students should not only be able to read graphs but also create them in order to display their data in clear and efficient ways.

During the instruction process, teachers should prompt students to look for patterns any time data are collected. It is especially important to remind a student that *not* finding a data pattern is also significant, as this means there is no recognizable relationship among the data collected.

Considering Lab Safety

As principal, you need to take your responsibility as the safety leader in your school seriously and be proactive. Staff should be trained in science safety on an annual basis. Since safety in the science classroom is complex and has many legal implications, your school system should employ someone knowledgeable who receives ongoing training in the changing laws and new hazards.

The following are some commonly asked questions about safety.

- **"What are class-size recommendations for science classes?"** The NSTA (2007a) advises no more than twenty-four students engaged in hands-on scientific activities in one class, because one teacher cannot safely supervise more students than that. Research shows that accidents rise dramatically as class enrollments exceed twenty-four or when not enough individual workspace is provided (West, Westerlund, Stephenson, & Nelson, 2005).

- **"What are the recommendations for personal safety equipment in the science classroom?"** The Occupational Safety and Health Administration (OSHA, 1974) and NSTA (2007b) state that school laboratories should include appropriate protective apparel for protection from the substances being handled.

- **"When should goggles be worn in a school laboratory?"** According to the American Chemical Society (ACS, 2003), goggles must be worn whenever anyone is handling chemicals, fire, projectiles (explosions and glassware), or compressed gas. Certain elementary and middle school science programs include these kinds of activities. Eye protection must meet the Industrial Eyewear Impact Standard for safety—ANSI Z87.1–2003. (American National Standards Institute [ANSI] is a nonprofit group that publishes standards for safety equipment.) Safety goggles must be worn during these situations at all times in a science lab. All individuals present in the lab, including visitors, must wear safety goggles, not safety glasses or spectacles (ACS, 2003).

- **"When can contact lenses be worn in a laboratory?"** Contact lenses can be worn in the laboratory, but they cannot provide adequate protection in situations involving chemical splashes (ACS, 2003). Always err on the side of caution and always have students wear protective goggles, regardless of whether or not contact lenses are being worn.

The OSHA Hazard Communication Standard (1987), more commonly called the *right-to-know laws*, states that people have the *right to know* about all hazards to which they are exposed in the workplace. Many hazards include flammability and the risk of toxicity by ingestion, inhalation, or skin contact, and most chemicals have some level of hazard associated with them. This standard states how hazard communication applies to school science facilities. In general, it requires the following.

- **Maintaining material safety data sheets (MSDS):** A primary source of information and communication on each chemical

- **Keeping a hazardous materials list:** Name, quantity, dangers (for example, corrosive, toxic, or combustible)

- **Cataloguing hazardous materials:** Name, quantity, and location

- **Notifying staff of hazardous materials:** MSDS and training

- **Training:** How to read labels, instruction on how to handle materials safely, and emergency procedures

- **Labeling hazardous materials:** With words like *corrosive, toxic,* or *combustible*

The Hazard Communication Standard for academic laboratories requires a chemical hygiene plan and a chemical hygiene officer. A chemical hygiene plan is a written report that includes: (1) laboratory regulations for personnel, equipment, and materials; (2) proper lab procedures for spills, storage, inspections, and training; and (3) instruction on how to respond to emergencies. These regulations are new to most people, which is why we recommend that when possible the school district hires a qualified person to guide school personnel in laboratory safety. Visit www.osha.gov and search Hazard Communication Standard to view all of the OSHA standards.

Flinn Scientific (2012; www.flinnsci.com/Sections/Safety/safety.asp) offers a wealth of information and resources on laboratory safety. Resources and topics include free science laboratory training videos, the Flinn material safety data sheet collection, general laboratory safety, chemical safety, eye and eyewear safety, safety contracts and exams, frequently asked safety questions, chemical storage, chemical disposal, charts for looking up chemicals students will be working with, and purchasing information. Additionally, ACS (2003) offers printed literature on rules and regulations for science laboratories, as well as literature that provides practical guidance in this area. The science lab setting presents many challenges for students with disabilities. Burgstahler (2009) does an exceptional job outlining accommodations for students with disabilities, such as using plastic labwear rather than glass for students with motor-skill impairments or pairing a student with special needs with a student who has fewer restrictions.

Establishing a Safe Learning Environment

Safety is a complex issue that often is ignored because it seems overwhelming. However, planning for safety is your responsibility. To begin, do the following.

1. Inventory chemicals and safety equipment. (Check your area for local companies that will come and properly inventory and dispose of dangerous or expired chemicals from classrooms or chemical storage closets).

2. Keep only the chemicals that you use and no more than a two-year supply.

3. Properly dispose of equipment and hazardous and nonhazardous materials that are not used.

4. Purchase approved safety equipment and storage containers.

5. Obtain and organize in alphabetical order all material safety data sheets.

6. Organize chemicals by compatible families, *not* alphabetical order.

7. Plan and organize safety training for all staff, including special education teachers and aides, that will be in lab settings.

> **NSTA Position Statement on Safety and School Science Instruction**
>
> **Preamble**
>
> Inherent in many instructional settings, including science, is the potential for injury and possible litigation. These issues can be avoided or reduced by the proper application of a safety plan.
>
> **Rationale**
>
> High-quality science instruction includes laboratory investigations, interactive or demonstration activities, and field trips.
>
> **Declarations**
>
> The National Science Teachers Association recommends that school districts and teachers adhere to the following guidelines.
>
> - School districts must adopt written safety standards that include hazardous material management and disposal procedures for chemical and biological wastes. These procedures must meet or exceed the standards adopted by the Environmental Protection Agency, OSHA, or appropriate state and local agencies.
> - School authorities and teachers share the responsibility of establishing and maintaining safety standards.
> - School authorities are responsible for providing safety equipment (like fire extinguishers), personal protective equipment (like eyewash stations and goggles), material safety data sheets, and appropriate training for each science teaching situation.
> - School authorities will inform teachers of the nature and limits of liability and tort insurance of the school district.
> - All science teachers must be involved in an established and ongoing safety training program relative to the established safety procedures, which is updated on an annual basis.
> - Teachers shall be notified of individual student health concerns.
> - The maximum number of occupants in a laboratory teaching space shall be based on the following:
>   a. Building and fire safety codes
>   b. Occupancy-load limits
>   c. Design of the laboratory teaching facility
>   d. Appropriate supervision and any special needs of students
> - Materials intended for human consumption shall not be permitted in any space used for hazardous chemicals or materials.
> - Students and parents will receive written notice of appropriate safety regulations to be followed in science instructional settings.
>
> *Source: NSTA, 2000b.*

Summary

To ensure that required science concepts are taught in school, you must develop an understanding of the standards, goals, benchmarks, objectives, and performance indicators for science achievement at each grade level; you must work with the teaching staff to determine on a quarterly basis when this content will be taught; you must make sure that the required content is taught appropriately; and you must find creative ways to support your staff.

These steps require that you work with your grade-level teams to squeeze the time out of their busy daily schedules to teach science. You need to find and enroll teachers in science professional development opportunities that provide them with the background knowledge and pedagogy necessary for them to feel comfortable teaching the required content for their grade levels. As a group, you also need to ascertain what materials, equipment, activities, and safety procedures teachers need at each grade level to adequately teach science in both the classroom and the lab. Science is not a passive subject and must include students doing hands-on activities, experimenting, and problem solving.

THREE
SCIENCE PROGRAM EVALUATION

As instructional leaders, principals are inundated with multiple tasks that frequently involve instruction in reading, writing, and arithmetic—the areas commonly assessed through the use of high-stakes tests. The standards and accountability movement rarely tests the value of inquiry, creativity, and higher-order thinking skills, all of which are integral components of science learning. This often leads to science instruction becoming a low priority for teachers. This should not be the case in a 21st century school.

Natural connections exist between the science curriculum and reading, writing, and doing mathematics. Because scientists read, write, and converse about science, language arts is integral to its study. Scientists analyze data, perform calculations, and generate reports, and conversely, all of these elements are essential components of curricula in other subjects. Teachers need to capitalize on the interdisciplinary connections inherent in science and make a conscientious effort to integrate the teaching of science with other subject matters. Principal leadership in this area is critical. Help your teachers, and work with them to see these interdisciplinary connections. Provide them with the support and resources necessary to integrate science into all areas of the curriculum.

How do you become an expert in an area in which you perhaps have spent the least amount of time and energy? You can begin by assessing your school's science progress with simple surveys and observations, developing a working knowledge of the science curriculum, identifying resources to assist you in developing your staff, enhancing your feedback to staff, and finding ways to involve stakeholders in the school's approach to science learning.

Science Program Self-Assessment Survey

School administrators, teachers, parents, and other stakeholders can complete a brief self-assessment survey, such as the reproducible "Science Program Self-Assessment Survey" on page 77 and online at **go.solution-tree.com/leadership**, to determine the strengths and weaknesses of a current K–8 science program. The survey covers science program content, assessment, teacher preparedness, school climate, and school system support. Figure 3.1 shows the portion of the survey on science program content.

Name: _____ **School:** _____

The survey is divided into five main categories: science program content, assessment, teacher preparedness, school climate, and school system support. Read the question in each section and rate them 1–5 according to the following scale:

1 = Poor, nonexistent, or never
2 = Low, rarely, or sometimes
3 = Medium, average, or half the time
4 = Above average, usually, or most of the time
5 = Excellent, continually, or almost all the time

Add your scores for all the surveys and then read the scenario that corresponds to your total score on pp. 33–36 of *What Principals Need to Know About Teaching and Learning Science*.

Science Program Content	Score 1–5
Does your school have a science program that lists overall goals, grade-level benchmarks, and individual behavior indicators for each course and grade?	
Does each grade level have a list of print materials, textbooks, library books, and supplemental activity sheets to support science instruction?	
Does each grade have a list of computer software, videos, DVDs, and so on that support science instruction?	
Does each grade level have a list of current websites that support science instruction?	
Does your school have a science laboratory or designated science area in the building to support and extend science instruction?	
Do you have a teacher who is highly qualified in science, or do you have training in the sciences for teachers?	
Does the curriculum address STEM initiatives and the importance of interdisciplinary connections?	
Total	

Figure 3.1: Sample science program self-assessment survey on science program content.

Stakeholders' results from the survey can be used collectively to determine if there is consensus in the school community with regard to the overall science instructional program. The data collected can also be used as a first step in developing an action plan for science instruction that builds on program strengths, integrates other disciplines, and emphasizes specific areas that can enhance student learning.

After your staff and administrators complete the self-assessment survey, tabulate the results. Analysis of the data will point you in the right direction. If you and your staff are in general agreement, you can proceed as an entire staff. If, on the other hand, you think improvement is needed and they do not, then you need to select a group of teachers with various opinions and form a committee to build a base of support before involving the whole staff. Change and continuous improvement are fun and exciting for some people, but not for others.

The results of the survey will provide you with data that you can share with your staff in small team or faculty meetings. Your presentation of the data should spark important conversations about the staff's interest in making science a schoolwide value.

Following are three scenarios with suggestions on how to proceed based on the outcome of the survey.

Scenario 1: Starting Your Science Program—25 to 50 Points

In this scenario, the survey has revealed that you do not have a clearly defined science program or an emphasis on STEM education. Your central office does not have any district-level science positions, or the person assigned to science wears many curriculum hats. Your school building has limited material resources, outdated textbooks, and minimal access to technology, and your classroom teachers do not have strong science knowledge backgrounds. To begin to turn this situation around, follow these ten steps.

1. Visit your state's department of education website and find the elementary science standards, benchmarks, and indicators. These are usually listed by grade level or by primary grades (K–3), upper elementary (grades 4–6), or middle school (grades 6–8). You can find a detailed list of such standards in appendix D (page 105).

2. Form a science subcommittee composed of teachers from each grade level. Ask them to compare what is currently being taught in science to what is supposed to be taught, as spelled out in your state standards.

3. Have the committee determine what resources are being used to teach the required content (for example, equipment, printed materials, media, and technology). The committee might enlist the aid of the school librarian.

4. Contact the state department of education science office or county equivalent and ask its representatives to furnish you with the names of school systems in your state that have model elementary and middle science programs.

5. Contact one or more of these school systems and find out what they are using and doing.

6. Work with the committee to develop an action plan of what can be done within three, six, and nine months to establish a science scope and sequence for each grade level. The scope and sequence map out what students need to know and when they need to know it in the science curriculum. (Note: It may take several years to phase in the curriculum and purchase the necessary materials.)

7. Present a nine-month plan of action to your faculty, and ask for feedback. (Be prepared for various stages of embracement as some staff fear change and extra work while others will be excited to enhance science instruction.)

8. Present the staff's plan to the parent-teacher association and the leadership of your school system to enlist monetary and, if possible, personnel support.

9. Start the plan. When you begin is optional, so begin at a time that is convenient.

10. Evaluate your progress approximately every three months, and refine your plan accordingly.

Refer to chapter 1 (page 5) for the national consensus on what scientists, educators, and researchers have found to be important aspects of exemplary curricula. Then, refer to chapter 2 for suggestions on science curricula (page 15).

Scenario 2: Developing Your Science Program—51 to 100 Points

The survey has shown that you have a science program for each grade level but limited materials to teach science. There are emerging connections to STEM principles. The central-office science designer wears many hats and visits your school infrequently. Your teachers are teaching science, but they lack quality assessment and evaluation strategies. Try the following nine steps.

1. Survey the staff and ask them to list the current ways they assess and evaluate science.

2. Collate the list, and work with the central office to select or add assessment strategies that can be used for each grade level.

3. Form a committee composed of one person per grade level to meet with you and the central science person. Familiarize each member of the committee with the list of assessments and evaluations. Have each committee member commit to try one or more of the strategies on the list within the next two weeks.

4. Reconvene the teacher group, and have each member report the positive and negative aspects of the assessment or evaluation he or she tried with students. Summarize the good ones, refine the average ones, and throw out the poor ones.

5. Have each committee member select another strategy and try it within the next two weeks. Meet again, and follow the same process. When you have two to four quality assessment strategies for each grade level, have the committee present them to the rest of the staff during a faculty meeting.

6. Provide coverage for the committee teachers so they can team teach with each other to model assessments and observe each other's instructional techniques. You can also serve as substitute for these teachers to provide them with this time.

7. Meet with the grade-level teams to assess what is working and other ideas they may have at their grade level for assessing and evaluating science instruction.

8. Award the committee teachers for their extra work. Recognition at a PTA function or with a restaurant or bookstore gift certificate is an affordable way to show appreciation.

9. Maintain files of assessment and evaluation strategies used at each grade level for specific science content. New strategies can be added to the file each year. This encourages teachers to share and can be a terrific resource for new teachers.

Refer to chapter 5 on assessment (page 55) and chapter 6 on professional development (page 67) for more strategies.

Scenario 3: Continuously Improving Your Science Program—101 to 125 Points

The survey results showed that you have a clearly defined science program that incorporates STEM principles and an accessible central-office science person. The school system provides you with adequate resources. Your teachers do a good job teaching, assessing, and evaluating science instruction. Your school's science test scores are average or above. You have an involved parent community that wants to see students excel in science. You want to improve the program so that a larger percentage of students achieves high grades, applies knowledge, and passes mandated state tests with higher scores. You might try the following ten steps.

1. Ask a teacher from each grade level to develop rubric assessments for activities in the units. Include student feedback in the development of these tools.

2. Distribute these rubrics to the students and their parents or guardians so that everyone is aware of the criteria needed to demonstrate learning and mastery of the content.

3. Ask teachers to use assessment strategies at the start of units to identify (1) students who will require additional time and resources to understand the content in a new unit, (2) students who will be able to master the content through normal instruction, and (3) students who know most of the content and need enrichment activities that add to their knowledge base.

4. Support teachers by creatively scheduling instructional aides to provide assistance during science lessons.

5. Arrange for people with science expertise to come to the school to present enrichment lessons to students.

6. Provide authentic learning experiences, such as field trips, independent study opportunities, and guest lecturers.

7. Purchase technology and equipment that will enhance science instruction.

8. Have each grade level design lesson plans and rubrics for a particular unit. After students have been evaluated, meet with each grade-level team to discuss the results. If the approach is successful, the materials can be shared.

9. Revise or refine your plans for the next science unit based on feedback from the unit evaluation meeting. Start the process again.

10. Highlight successes and share ideas for improving science instruction at meetings (such as faculty, PTA, and board of education meetings). Communicate innovations through email blasts, newsletters, and social media (like blogs, Twitter, Facebook, and so on).

Other Data Worth Considering

In addition to the self-assessment survey data, it would be wise to pull together other data to help you show staff and stakeholders how your students are doing in their science learning. The following is a list of other data to consider.

- **Student grades:** If you were to collectively analyze all of the grades on student report cards, you might find patterns worthy of staff discussion. Why is every student earning high marks in science? What criteria are used to determine grades? Are these grades reflective of scientific inquiry and applications? Do they adequately ascertain student learning and growth? Or do they simply reflect reading comprehension skills or the attractiveness of a project?

- **Standardized test scores:** Despite criticism of the ability of standardized tests to truly measure development of scientific thinking, these scores are highly publicized and the public considers them to represent student achievement in science. Even if your scores are high, it is worth the time to study their true meaning. Are the students merely recalling knowledge, or are they applying their knowledge in authentic, scientific ways? For newer standardized tests, there is usually a balance between recall and application. If the test aligns with the values of inquiry and scientific methodology, then you may espouse your scores as indicators of your science goals. If the test measures reading comprehension in the area of science content, it is important to teach your staff and parent community what methods of evaluation you wish to use to better inform them of your definition of science achievement.

- **Participation in science events:** It is worthwhile to document the ways in which students participate in scientific events. You may wish to analyze the number of students who participated in the local or state science fair or to recognize the number of students who participated in Science Olympiad or middle school Science Bowl competitions. Another option is to document the number of field trips or student assemblies that are science related. Visit http://cty.jhu.edu/imagine/resources/competitions/science.html for a listing of other national science competitions.

- **Master schedule:** You may wish to analyze the number of hours per week used to teach science and the time of day that seems to be most effective for science learning. For example, do you find that classes that have science after recess tend to do better than those that have it before? This will vary from school to school, and as the educational leader, you need to look at these numbers and determine what would work best for your school. These data can serve as an impetus for schoolwide goal setting and the establishment of priorities surrounding staff and community values for science instruction.

Summary

Science instruction has been brought to the forefront of education-reform debates. As a result, there is a more concerted effort to emphasize the importance of science education fueled by STEM initiatives (Anderson et al., 2011). Elements of STEM are integral components of our economy, from health care and infrastructure needs to energy and the environment (Metz, 2011). In November 2009, President Barack Obama launched the Educate to Innovate campaign, a nationwide effort to help move U.S. students from the middle to the top of the pack in science achievement by 2020. In his announcement, the president stressed the importance of "reaffirming and strengthening America's role as the world's engine of scientific discovery and technological innovation" to meet the challenges of the 21st century (The White House, Office of the Press Secretary, 2009). However, the reality is that our schools fall way behind other countries when it comes to STEM education. As Venkataraman, Riordan, and Olson (2010) note:

> Despite our historical record of achievement, the United States now lags behind other nations in STEM education at the elementary and secondary levels. International comparisons of our students' performance in science and mathematics consistently place the United States in the middle of the pack or lower. (p. 8)

How students think scientifically and ethically will be vital to every foreseeable role they will play in our society. The time has come to focus on K–8 curriculum that develops scientific thinking and understanding and that places a greater emphasis on STEM.

FOUR
INQUIRY-BASED LEARNING

For students to build science connections, teachers must deliver instruction in a manner that helps learners construct their own knowledge by building connections among topics and across disciplines. An unconnected lesson that does not allow students to demonstrate or apply what they have learned is not an effective lesson. The role of an instructional leader is to identify the pedagogical techniques and strategies that are being employed through the use of observation, walkthroughs, and probing questions about the science that is being taught, and to collaboratively discuss them with teachers. The following questions can serve as a guide for principals to ascertain whether or not their teachers are teaching for deep understanding and application of knowledge:

- What is the objective of today's lesson?
- How does it build on what you taught during the previous science lesson?
- How does it build on what you will teach during the next science lesson?
- How do the science concepts taught today connect and support the science being taught in the unit?
- How will students apply what they have learned?

An informal interview using these essential questions will allow you to gauge the degree to which teachers are providing meaningful and effective instruction. It will offer you an opportunity to sit down and discuss strategies for teaching science with the teachers. A sample reproducible form, "Reflective Discussion Guidelines," is located on page 79 (and online at **go.solution-tree.com/leadership**). This interview is not intended to replace your classroom observations of teachers; rather, it is meant to help you and the teacher develop a deeper understanding of how science is taught and how science teaching can be improved throughout your school.

Supporting Teachers in Planning for Science Instruction

When planning a unit or lesson, teachers must first plan what is going to be taught and then plan how they are going to teach and assess learning. It is essential that principals engage each staff member responsible for teaching science in conversations focused on effective planning. These conversations should not only assist the teacher in planning well-structured lessons but also in creating a variety of assessments that can measure and identify conceptual learning. Specifically, principals need to make sure teachers are doing the following.

- Collaboratively identifying specifically what students are to learn (big idea, essential knowledge, important knowledge, and what's worth knowing)

- Informing students about what they are to learn by distributing objectives in writing or displaying them during the lesson

- Teaching what students are to learn; it is a sound educational practice to write the objective of each lesson on the board so that students have a constant reminder of where the lesson is going and what they are expected to learn. (See pages 80–81 for the reproducible guides "Planning to Teach for Understanding I" and "Planning to Teach for Understanding II.")

- Planning the assessment of student understanding; teachers should also identify how students will demonstrate their understanding of the content.

Providing Assessment Support

To provide constructive feedback, to engage teachers in conversations on improvement, and to promote reflection, principals must have an understanding of how children learn science. Teachers should feel comfortable and confident turning to principals for instructional guidance, support, and feedback. It is also important for principals during conferences to remain supportive of the teachers' efforts and provide justifications for specific suggestions. Understand that change takes time and that immediate improvement may not be forthcoming.

Signs of Ineffective Science Instruction

The main purpose of observing teachers is to ensure that students are receiving high-quality, effective instruction in a safe, supportive, and engaging environment. The reproducible "Direct Observation Inventory" (page 82) will provide you with information on the type of instruction that is taking place. As you observe teachers and engage them in reflective conversations about their science instruction, you will learn a great deal about their strengths, weaknesses, and comfort levels with instructional practices and specific material. Teacher observations and the follow-up discussions should be used to help teachers become better at the craft of teaching. "Indicators of Ineffective Science Instruction" (page 84) will assist you.

In spite of the best efforts of teachers, administrators, and professional developers, some science instruction is uninformed by best practices research. The reproducibles "Observation

Guidelines" (pages 85–89) list guidelines for effective K–8 science instruction at the classroom and building levels. Principals should keep these guidelines in mind as they observe staff teaching science. They can also function as a springboard for discussion among teachers about best practices.

Collaboration With Teachers to Improve Science Instruction

Principals can work with teachers in a number of ways to improve science teaching. Consider the following.

- Facilitate the development of a schedule that allows for peer observations. Encourage teachers at the same grade level to observe science lessons in each other's classrooms. There is a great deal to be learned from watching others teach and then discussing what was observed. Teachers who are in need of support may find peer observations less threatening than administrator observations.

- If you cannot facilitate the development of a peer-observation schedule, try to incorporate a common planning period for teachers of the same subject. Having peers teaching the same subject with the same prep period will encourage teacher collaboration on projects that utilize best practices. Once a month you may want to join teachers during a common planning period to facilitate and offer guidance on developing an inquiry-based lesson or new lab or project.

- Provide staff development offerings, such as workshops or seminars, in needed areas. For example, if you begin to notice that many teachers are not able to adequately monitor student progress, you might organize a staff development session on approaches to science assessment. However, it is often not cost effective for a school to bring in just a science specialist; if that is the case, allow teachers to search out seminars or professional development sessions outside of your district and allow professional leave days in order for them to attend. This will expand your professional development offerings and allow you to suggest seminars that are geared more toward individual teachers.

- Ask the science curriculum specialist to observe a science lesson in the teacher's classroom and to provide constructive feedback and ideas for improvement. The curriculum specialist could also teach a lesson to the teacher's class, with the teacher observing.

- Record the teacher teaching a lesson or series of lessons, and then watch and critique the video together. Be sure to point out positives in addition to negatives, so teachers don't feel discouraged after leaving your office.

- Provide the teacher with a list of resources, such as books or Internet sites, to which he or she can refer for lesson ideas, instructional strategies, or topical information.

- Arrange articulation meetings between science teachers at different levels to discuss shortcomings or areas where students are excelling. Having meetings with science teachers at all levels allows teachers to discuss student progress and explore ways that teachers can work together to develop 21st century science students.

- Arrange articulation meetings to discuss curriculum and what students are expected to know at each level.

The staff development offerings discussed in chapter 6 are another way to help teachers develop their knowledge and skills.

Promoting Inquiry-Based Teaching

Inquiry-based teaching has been found to have a significant impact on student learning. This is not only how scientists conduct science but also how students learn science most effectively. Farenga, Joyce, and Dowling (2002) note, "The process of inquiry requires students to follow a somewhat linear process, which includes identifying a question, designing an investigation, developing a hypothesis, collecting data, answering and modifying the original question, and communicating their results" (p. 34). Research has shown that students involved in research-based inquiries develop more sophisticated levels of intellectual development (Baxter Magolda, 1999; Blackmore & Cousin, 2003). Inquiry-based teaching fosters scientific curiosity in children. According to the National Science Education Standards (NRC, 1996):

> Scientific inquiry refers to the diverse ways in which scientists study the natural world and propose explanations based on the evidence derived from their work. Inquiry also refers to the activities of students in which they develop knowledge and understanding of scientific ideas, as well as an understanding of how scientists study the natural world.
>
> Inquiry is a multifaceted activity that involves making observations; posing questions; examining books and other sources of information to see what is already known; planning investigations; reviewing what is already known in light of experimental evidence; using tools to gather, analyze, and interpret data; proposing answers, explanations, and predictions; and communicating the results. Inquiry requires identification of assumptions, use of critical and logical thinking, and consideration of alternative explanations. (p. 23)

You can find content standards for science as inquiry in appendix D (page 105).

Effective Hands-On Learning

Students are central to the inquiry process in the classroom. They should be engaged in making observations, formulating then asking questions, analyzing evidence, evaluating data, formulating explanations, connecting their explanations with scientific concepts, and communicating the justification for their explanations. This process takes time, as students and teachers build their skills and comfort level with the inquiry process. In districts with well-planned science curricula, students are exposed to this type of learning starting in kindergarten, so that they build their inquiry skills over time.

Research suggests that the constructivist (question-based) learning cycle may be helpful in guiding science instruction, as it engages students through a cyclical process that has them sequentially explore, construct explanations, and apply what they have learned to new situations (Cakir, 2008; Trowbridge, Bybee, & Powell, 2000). Questions drive the learning cycle, whether the questions are used to enhance learning or to assess understanding.

Effective hands-on science is described as students manipulating real science materials, when safe and appropriate, in ways that scientists do. The NSTA (2007a) recommends that students should spend more than half of their science time engaged in hands-on science. To more fully understand hands-on science, let's look at some examples.

Is observing plastic models of animals hands-on? No, because scientists study living animals. While plastic models may be clean and easily observed, they do not excite and engage the students. Rather than show students a video on insect structure, go outside and collect some bugs. Make the experience as authentic as possible, so students get a feel for how science is conducted.

Is conducting a computer simulation of a pendulum hands-on science? No, but creating an activity using a string and a mass can easily be done in the classroom. When we eliminate the hands-on step and go directly to computer simulations, students do not internalize and remember the scientific content. However, even though the computer simulation is not considered hands-on science, it can be an effective tool for learning. An emphasis should be placed on first engaging students in hands-on science and then extending the experience through simulations. Hands-on science activities should comprise a minimum of 50 percent of the allotted instructional time. This still allows for a variety of student-centered activities to be used to promote inquiry, critical thought, and learning. Simulations can be one of these other activities.

Is exploring satellite weather data or images of Mars on a computer hands-on science? Yes, because this is what scientists do. Teachers should explain to students that although we can't personally go to Mars or view its weather, we can use a computer to look at the same data that scientists study for information about the planet and its weather. Some great sites principals can refer their teachers to are Google Mars (www.google.com/mars), Google Earth 5: Explore Mars (http://earth.google.com/mars), and NASA's Interactive Mars Data Maps (http://marsoweb.nas.nasa.gov/globalData).

Teachers who have never used inquiry-based methods may be skeptical or nervous about implementing them. This is where, as a leader, you can collaborate and offer insights into designing a lesson. Assist your teachers, and offer them the tools and insight they need to successfully integrate inquiry-based lessons into their classroom. For example, you could allow teachers to apply for a professional leave day to go observe a teacher in another school or district who implements inquiry-based methods effectively on a routine basis. Table 4.1 (page 44) shows the essential features of classroom inquiry.

Table 4.1: Essential Features of Classroom Inquiry and Variations

Essential Feature	Variations			
Learner engages in scientifically oriented questions.	Learner poses a question.	Learner selects among questions; poses new questions.	Learner sharpens or clarifies question the teacher, materials, or other source provides.	Learner engages in answering question the teacher, materials, or other source provides.
Learner gives priority to evidence in responding to questions.	Learner determines what constitutes evidence and collects it.	Learner collects certain data based on teacher advice.	Learner analyzes given data.	Learner is told how to analyze given data.
Learner formulates explanations from evidence.	Learner formulates explanations after summarizing evidence.	Learner follows teacher's process of formulating explanations from evidence.	Learner formulates explanation after being given possible ways.	Learner formulates explanation after being provided with evidence.
Learner connects explanations to scientific knowledge.	Learner examines other resources independently and forms the links to explanations.	Learner is directed toward areas and sources of scientific knowledge.	Learner is given possible connections.	Learner is given the connections.
Learner communicates and justifies explanations.	Learner forms reasonable and logical argument to communicate explanations.	Learner develops communication through coaching.	Learner follows broad guidelines to sharpen communication.	Learner follows steps and procedures for communication.
	More ◄——— Amount of learner self-direction ———► Less			
	Less ◄——— Amount of direction from teacher or material ———► More			

Source: Reprinted with permission from National Academies Press, Copyright 2000, National Academy of Sciences.

Is all hands-on learning inquiry based? The quick answer is no. Much of what we observe in a struggling teacher's classroom is students "playing" with materials. Free exploration is a good first step, but it needs to have a purpose and be guided with questions.

As the instructional leader, you should ask teachers questions such as, "What is the purpose of the activity?" When you receive vague answers such as, "The students are exploring," probe further by asking, "For what purpose?" "What is the objective of the exploration?" and "How does this activity connect to other disciplines?"

Strategies to Improve Student Achievement in Science

Many teaching practices augment and support inquiry-based science teaching. However, these need to be selected and implemented systematically and in ways that support hands-on, inquiry-based science instruction and the multiple learning styles of students.

Questioning Strategies That Promote Critical Thought

Since questions drive the inquiry process, teachers should understand effective questioning techniques, as well as strategies for increasing student responses and calling on students. Questions can be analyzed in terms of hierarchical levels using Bloom's Taxonomy as a guide. Within this system, questions are classified as one of six types: (1) knowledge, (2) comprehension, (3) application, (4) analysis, (5) synthesis, or (6) evaluation. Since these levels are hierarchical from lower- to higher-order thinking, they give an indication of the level of question being asked. Research shows that teachers ask mainly lower-order-thinking questions—that is, those at the knowledge, comprehension, and application levels (Moore & Stanley, 2010). As you engage teachers in reflective conversation about professional practice, encourage them to pose questions that also require analysis, synthesis, and evaluation, for example:

- Why did the changes occur?
- Why did that reaction happen in the experiment?
- How can you identify through song the components and characteristics of the scientific method?
- What would happen if a plant did not receive enough sunlight?
- How effective are pesticides at protecting crops?
- How would you feel if every tree was cut down?

Many state-administered standardized science tests are moving away from the recall-type questioning and toward the analysis-, synthesis-, and evaluation-type questioning that requires students to not only understand the material but also be able to apply information to specific tasks.

Laboratory Science in Elementary and Middle School

For science to be taught properly and effectively, labs must be an integral part of the science curriculum. The NSTA (2007a) recommends that all science teachers provide instruction with a priority on making observations and gathering evidence, much of which students experience in the lab or the field, to help students develop a deep understanding of the science content, as well as an understanding of the nature of science, the attitudes of science, and the skills of scientific reasoning. The following are recommendations for K–8 laboratory science instruction (NSTA, 2007a).

Preschool and Elementary School

- With schools' expectation for science instruction to take place every day, all students at the preschool and elementary levels should receive multiple opportunities every week to explore science labs (NSTA, 2007a).

- Laboratory investigations should allow students the opportunity to explore familiar phenomena and materials. At age-appropriate levels, learners should investigate appropriate questions, analyze the results of lab-based investigations, debate what the evidence means, construct an understanding of science concepts, and apply these concepts to the world around them (NSTA, 2007a).

- A minimum of 60 percent of science instruction time should be devoted to hands-on activities in which learners are investigating, manipulating, observing, exploring, and inquiring about science using concrete materials. Reading, computer programs, and teacher demonstrations are valuable, but they should not be substituted for hands-on science experiences (NSTA, 2007a, 2007b).

- Evaluation and assessment of student performance should reflect hands-on experience.

- Hands-on activities should be supported with a yearly building science budget, including a petty-cash fund for immediate materials purchase, due to the fact that some items are perishable and cannot be purchased in advance. Proper amounts of supplies and equipment that are used on a routine basis—like magnets, microscopes, cells, slides, and so on—should be purchased and stocked, permitting each child to have a hands-on learning experience. Many science activities can also be taught using easily accessible, free, and inexpensive materials.

- Appropriate and necessary safety precautions should always be taken when teachers and students are interacting with manipulative materials, especially those that are potentially harmful.

- Preschool and elementary science should be taught in a classroom with sufficient workspace to include flat moveable desks or tables, chairs, equipment, and hands-on materials. Consideration should be made for purchase and storage of materials with convenient accessibility to water and electricity. Computers, software, and other electronic tools should be available for children's use as an integral part of science activities.

- Parents, community resource people, and PTA members should be enlisted to assist preschool and elementary teachers with science activities and experiences. For example, these individuals could act in the role of field-trip chaperones, science fair assistants, material collectors, or science classroom aides. Also, many parents have access to materials at their jobs and are willing to donate materials (for example, contractors will have scrap wood, glass, or screen, and doctors are usually willing to donate gloves or other minor supplies).

- The number of children assigned to each class should not exceed twenty-four. Teachers and students must have immediate access to each other in order to provide a safe and effective learning environment.

- Some schools have the luxury of having a science lab in the building that interested teachers can reserve. These labs should have ideal setups for cooperative lab groups and necessary materials for lab experiences.

Middle School

- All middle school students should have multiple opportunities every week to explore science labs (NSTA, 2007a).

- Middle school laboratory investigations should develop learners' conceptual understanding of the complexity and ambiguity of empirical work, as well as the skills required to calibrate and troubleshoot equipment used to make observations. Learners should understand measurement error and have the skills to aggregate, interpret, and present the resulting data (NSTA, 2007a).

- A minimum of 70 percent of the science instruction time should be allocated to laboratory-related experiences. This time includes prelab instruction in concepts relevant to the laboratory, hands-on student activities, and postlab questions involving the analysis and communication of results.

- Technology resources such as digital media, computer simulations, and teacher demonstrations are valuable but should not be substitutions for laboratory activities.

- Investigations should be relevant to authentic issues in science, technology, engineering, and mathematics. In those schools in which team teaching is practiced, science topics should be integrated with the other curricular areas for a fully integrated interdisciplinary learning experience.

- Evaluation and assessment of student achievement in science should be differentiated in order to reflect the full range of student experiences, especially laboratory activities.

- An adequate budget for facilities, equipment, and supplies should be provided to support the laboratory activities. The budget needs to provide funds for the purchase of needed laboratory materials throughout the course of the school year.

- Teachers should be provided with training in laboratory safety on an annual basis. Principals must ensure that the necessary safety equipment, such as safety goggles, fire extinguishers, and eyewashes, are provided and maintained on a routine basis.

- The number of students assigned to each class should not exceed twenty-four. Continuous access to each student is an imperative component of sustaining a safe and stimulating learning environment.

Models

Models are an effective mechanism for advancing scientific thought and understanding. According to the AAAS (1993), "Physical, mathematical, and conceptual models are tools for learning about the things they are meant to resemble. Physical models are by far the most obvious to young children, so they should be used to introduce the idea of models" (p. 267). Toys—such as Legos, K'Nex, Play-Doh, and Bendaroos—often provide useful physical models for starting discussions with children (Checkovich & Sterling, 2001).

As children advance through elementary school, models can be introduced to represent physical phenomena and processes that are too small, large, fast, or slow to observe directly, as well as to represent abstract ideas. For example, children can draw what they see in a microscope or sketch a map of a stream where they collected data. These models are especially helpful for discussing abstract concepts or remembering details. Scientists use sketches, diagrams, maps, graphs, and other types of models to record observations and explain abstract concepts. Research has shown that models are powerful tools teachers can use to diagnose conceptual misunderstandings of students (AAAS, 1993; Armstrong, 1994; Gardner, 1983; Hestenes, 1996).

Authentic Best Practices of Science Teaching

Engaging resilient preconceptions (addressing students' initial understanding and preconceptions about topics): Students do not come into the classroom as a *tabula rasa*—they are not blank sheets to be written on. Each student comes into the classroom with ideas that often limit what he or she can learn. It is critical that student preconceptions be identified, confronted, and resolved.

Supporting metacognition and student self-regulation (teaching strategies that will help students take control of their learning): Students need to be made fully aware of what they know and what they don't know. This can often be accomplished by requiring students to summarize what they have learned. Alternatively, the use of a sample test or a pretest can be used to help students become more aware of what they know and don't know. Socratic dialogues can be used to the same end. There are many heuristics that can be used to help students self-assess and then self-regulate.

Organizing knowledge around core concepts (providing a foundation of factual knowledge and conceptual knowledge): Organizing information can be a powerful way to increase understanding and retention. For instance, recognizing a pattern can be a powerful adjunct to retrieval. If you were to ask a student to memorize the following list of numbers, he or she would have a difficult time unless the underlying pattern was made visible: 13, 7, 19, 10, 4, 1, 25, 16, 22, and 28. If the pattern is made clear by essentially rearranging the information, a rule can readily be established so remembering the sequence is very easy: 1, 4, 7, 10, 13, 16, 19, 22, 25, and 28. The rule is, "Starting with 1, add three until you reach 28." A few core concepts of physics are conservation of energy, momentum, charge, and matter. These are some of the big ideas identified in the National Science Education Standards. Similarly, students should receive direct instruction to come to know how the problem-solving process is conducted rather than through learning by example. Appendix E (page 109) provides an elementary example of organizing knowledge around the core concepts.

Employing cooperative learning: Using cooperative learning for classroom and laboratory instruction increases student achievement, attitudes, and on-task behavior and can also keep supply costs lower than they would be if you were to have students work individually. This should not be confused with group learning—there are huge differences. Cooperative learning calls for PIGS FACE: positive interdependence, individual accountability, group processing, social skills, and face-to-face interaction. Laboratory activities provide a fantastic opportunity to incorporate cooperative learning. To ensure students remain on task and are held accountable for work completed, teachers should assign individual roles (for example, the materials manager, time keeper, recorder, and safety manager). For a plethora of resources on cooperative learning, visit Instructional Strategies Online (http://olc.spsd.sk.ca/DE/PD/instr/strats/coop).

Source: Donovan & Bransford, 2005.

Concept Maps

Concept maps are effective tools for helping students identify connections and relationships. Additionally, they allow teachers to develop insights into student thinking. When developing a concept map, the main concept is placed at the top or center. Related concepts are then linked to it with lines between the concepts describing the relationships and representing connections. Concept maps can be simple or complex and can be made for group or individual projects. A great website to use for creating concept maps is bubbl (www.bubbl.us). Your teachers can use this web-based application to create a concept map for the class, and students can also use it to create their own. As students develop their understanding of a concept, like *photosynthesis*, they add cross links that connect plant growth to water, air, and sunlight.

Literacy Processes

Reading and writing are fundamental components of scientific literacy (Norris & Phillips, 2003). Talking, writing, and reading all play important roles in science learning (Pegg, 2010). The processes of scientific inquiry—such as questioning, hypothesizing, gathering and organizing data, drawing conclusions, analyzing results, and reporting—are similar to the literacy processes of purpose setting, predicting, organizing ideas, constructing and composing, evaluating and revising, and comprehending and communicating (Baker, 2004). Students can read instructions, discuss and record observations, and write conclusions based on their science investigations. Hands-on, inquiry-based science provides multiple opportunities to develop skills in these areas.

Moreover, research has shown that integrating reading and writing into content-area instruction can lead to improved student achievement in science and language arts (Pegg, 2010). The purpose of reading should always be to find information for a specific reason, not just to cover the material. To increase comprehension, prereading activities should build on prior knowledge and establish a purpose for reading to enhance understanding. In addition, reading about current events, role models, and careers can increase the relevance for students of the science being studied (Sterling, 1996; Wilson, 1995). Science Notebooks in K–12 Classrooms (http://sciencenotebooks.org) is a great resource teachers can use to incorporate writing and critical-thinking skills into science instruction.

NSTA Position Statement on Quality Education and 21st Century Skills

Preamble
Rapid changes in the world—including technological advancement, scientific innovation, increased globalization, shifting workforce demands, and pressures of economic competitiveness—are redefining the broad skill sets that students need to be adequately prepared to participate in and contribute to today's society (Levy & Murnane, 2004; Stewart, 2010; Wilmarth, 2010).

Rationale
NSTA acknowledges the need for and importance of 21st century skills within the context of science education and advocates for the science education community to support 21st century skills consistent with best practices across a preK–16 science education system.

continued →

> **Declarations**
> - Science leaders cultivate 21st century skills that best align to good science teaching.
> - Science instruction aligns with the National Science Education Standards, Benchmarks for Science Literacy, Science Framework for the 2011 National Assessment of Educational Progress, and Science College Board Standards for College Success.
> - Students meet the standards for scientific inquiry and technological design.
> - Students have a complete, accurate, and working understanding of the nature of science.
> - Ongoing professional development opportunities and effective preservice and induction programs for science educators support the integration of 21st century skills in classroom teaching.
> - Quality inquiry-based curricula and support materials promote science learning and 21st century skills.
> - Assessments are aligned with 21st century curriculum and instruction, and appropriately measure students' progress toward skills acquisition in addition to mastery of core content.
> - A wide range of technologies serves as a tool to engage students with real-world problem solving, conceptual development, and critical thinking.
> - Instruction includes a variety of opportunities for students to investigate and build scientific explanations, such as laboratory experiences.
> - Science leaders build on the opportunities that already exist in school programs and teaching practices to support 21st century skills.
>
> *Source: NSTA, 2011a.*

Technology

Computer or cloud-based word processing (like Google Docs), spreadsheets, presentation, and web 2.0 tools can enhance the way students and teachers investigate and learn about science concepts. However, technology also has more specific applications for science (Priest & Sterling, 2001). Appendix B (page 95) has online resources for common science technology.

Teachers can easily enhance the process of collecting data using science probeware—any educational software or hardware used to collect real-time data that can be displayed on a calculator or computer. This allows teachers to view data as they are collected. For example, temperature or pH probes can be used to collect temperature and acidity data to compare two streams before and after they merge. Research has found that the consistent use of probeware in the science classroom results in significant learning gains (Zuker, Tinker, Staudt, Manfield, & Metcalf, 2008).

Scientists share their data with colleagues around the world. Scientists also depend on data from one another in order to collect larger samples for better results. Teachers in different classes, schools, states, or countries can contribute data in one spreadsheet for student analysis. Shared, web-based spreadsheet programs such as Google Docs can open the world to students and allow sharing of data for students to analyze. This is another way students can see how scientists actually work.

Simulations can be powerful learning tools when selectively chosen. In addition to simulation software, simulations can easily be found on the Internet. The most effective simulations are animated and interactive. PhET (http://phet.colorado.edu) has some fantastic simulations for K–8 science teachers. Appendix B (page 95) has a detailed list of simulations.

Real science data sets can also be found on the Internet. This is an exciting way to make science relevant and up to date for students. When engaged in a unit on weather, students can look at satellite images of the current weather systems and interpret the same data that scientists use (Sterling, 2002). Looking at real-world data, such as satellite images, often enhances students' interest in learning and science. The Internet can also be used to make science more relevant and meaningful to students by making connections to news and current events. Sites such as Science News (www.sciencenews.org) and Science News for Kids (www.sciencenewsforkids.org) are great resources to spark student inquiry and increase engagement.

Blogging is another way for students to use technology that can tie into the language arts component mentioned. Using a website such as www.blogger.com can allow teachers to set up blogs for their classrooms so students can publish their thoughts. Consider supporting your teachers in the use of a blogging platform for students to use in submitting their lab reports. This will enhance essential skills, such as communication and collaboration, as both the teacher and other students can comment on the results.

Possibly one of the most powerful tools available to K–8 science teachers is the interactive whiteboard. Whether it is a SMART or Promethean whiteboard, this type of technology can increase student engagement and assist with the learning of science concepts. Interactive whiteboards also allow science teachers to adequately address the multiple learning styles of their respective students, especially those who learn best through tactile and visual learning activities. Specific interactive whiteboard links and resources can be found in appendix B (page 95).

Globally Enhancing the Science Classroom

Many students are sheltered within their own geographic region. Things that exist outside of their area are often foreign and difficult for them to understand. Encouraging global interaction and tying in real-world data from around the globe can enhance a science lesson greatly. There are various ways to do that.

Encouraging your teachers to think outside of the box—and outside of the region—is a great way to help them incorporate new strategies into old lessons. Unfortunately, many teachers think that using new strategies or working with teachers from other places is too difficult. Social media provides a gateway to expand learning opportunities beyond the walls of your school. Consider showing your staff how easy it can be to collaborate with other teachers from around the world using social media.

The Internet offers endless possibilities with regard to collaboration. One of the most useful connection tools that educators can use is Twitter (www.twitter.com), a social networking and blogging service that allows individuals to connect and share with one another in 140 characters or less. By simply searching for *science teachers*, an individual can connect with science teachers from all corners of the globe. Another powerful collaboration and connection tool is the Educator's PLN (http://edupln.ning.com). The Educator's PLN is like Facebook but is used exclusively for teachers looking to connect and share their ideas with other teachers around the world.

Video conferencing is a way that teachers can bring in various people from around the world without ever leaving the classroom. Video conferencing allows teachers to connect with other teachers, once an initial connection has been made, or to chat with a scientist or researcher studying a topic that students are currently investigating. A great, free video-chatting tool is Skype (www.skype.com). Skype allows you to make video calls around the world free of charge. It even has a learning community (http://education.skype.com), where teachers can connect with each other or classes from all over the world. A similar feature is available through Google Talk (http://talk.google.com), which opens a video chat box right in your browser window. Apple also offers a program called iChat, which is preinstalled on most MacBooks and Mac desktops.

Students should understand that science is often a collaborative effort. Many scientific studies and projects are done on a global scale (like the Human Genome Project), and this approach can be applied to projects done in your teachers' classrooms. Perhaps they could conduct a study of climate from around the United States, having students input data into a shared spreadsheet so all teachers can edit and view the information. Google Docs (http://docs.google.com) allows users to create free online documents that can be shared and added to. Another program called Dropbox (www.dropbox.com) allows users to share any document with others and save to one common document. Both of these programs facilitate successful collaboration.

Research-Supported Practices

Analogies: Using analogies in science teaching results in the development of conceptual understanding by enabling the learner to compare something familiar with something unfamiliar.

Wait time: Pausing after asking a question in the classroom results in an increase in achievement.

Concept mapping: The use of student-generated and teacher-generated concept maps for teaching science concepts results in improved student achievement and more positive student attitudes.

Computer simulations: Using computer simulations to represent real-world situations enables students to become more reflective problem solvers and to increase their conceptual understanding.

Microcomputer-based laboratories: Using computers to collect and display data from science experiments enables students at the secondary level to understand science concepts and learn to use science process skills.

Systematic approaches in problem solving: Planning the solutions to mathematics, chemistry, and physics problems in a systematic way enables students to more frequently solve the problems correctly.

> **Conceptual understanding in problem solving:** Understanding concepts qualitatively enables students to more effectively solve quantitative problems in biology, physics, and chemistry.
>
> **Science, technology, and society:** Using an inquiry-driven technology, and society approach in science teaching results in an increase in the number of students taking additional science courses and advanced-level courses, as well as changing students' attitudes toward science and their understanding of the nature of science and its relationship to technology and societal issues.
>
> **Real-life situations:** Using real-life situations in science instruction through the use of technology (films, DVDs, streaming video, virtual field trips, Skype) or through actual observation increases student interest in science, problem-solving skills, and achievement.
>
> **Discrepant events:** Using discrepant events in science instruction results in cognitive conflict that enhances students' conceptual understanding and students' attitudes toward critical-thinking activities.
>
> *Source: Educational Research Service, 1999, p. 6.*

Summary

Inquiry-based learning is a key component of effective science instruction. All science teachers should implement inquiry-based learning throughout the course of the year in each of their science classes. As a principal, you should become versed in this practice and encourage your teachers to become comfortable with it as well. Infusing the class with authentic data and scientific findings and practices will also help engage students and increase their interest. In turn, that will raise their levels of achievement.

FIVE
ASSESSMENT

Assessments are needed to monitor student progress in understanding the material. In addition to assessing students, teachers can also use assessments to evaluate their own teaching. There are many forms of assessment beside tests, as we'll explain in this chapter, and teachers should explore different types in order to best gauge understanding.

Assessment is a multistep process that should inform decision making at all levels. Systematic and ongoing data collection and interpretation serve as a guide to practice and policy decisions for effective education.

To begin the assessment process, you must identify the purposes for which data will be collected and the many ways in which they will be used. It is then necessary to specify the types of data to be collected, the ways they will be collected, and who will use them. The following are examples of (1) data use, (2) data collection, (3) data-collection methods, and (4) data users. These four components can be combined in numerous ways, leading to a decision based on that information. The variety of uses, users, methods, and data contributes to the complexity of the assessment process.

1. **Data use:**
    - Plan teaching
    - Guide learning
    - Make comparisons
    - Ensure credentials and licensure
    - Determine access to special or advanced education
    - Develop education theory
    - Inform policy formulation

- Monitor effects of policy
- Allocate resources
- Evaluate quality of curricula, programs, and teaching practices

2. **Data collection:**
   - To describe and quantify
     - Student achievement and attitude
     - Teacher preparation and quality
     - Program characteristics
     - Resource allocation
     - Policy instruments

3. **Data-collection methods:**
   - Pencil-and-paper testing
   - Performance testing
   - Interviews
   - Portfolios
   - Benchmark performance assessments
   - Program, student, and teacher observation
   - Transcript analysis
   - Expert reviews of educational materials
   - Lab practicals

4. **Data users:**
   - Teachers
   - Students
   - Educational administrators
   - Parents
   - Public
   - Policymakers
   - Institutions of higher education
   - Business and industry
   - Government

Because assessment of student progress is key to ensuring that instruction is both on target and effective, a school's assessment activities should be a carefully planned component of its instructional framework. By using carefully developed and selected assessments, schools can ensure that the science instruction provided is synchronized with diverse student needs.

Assessments to Evaluate Science Learning

By choosing assessments that match the purposes of testing, teachers and administrators have an increased chance of obtaining revealing information that will enhance teaching and learning. In order to fully assess students and make the best educational decisions based on their needs, a mixture of formal and informal assessment methods should be used. Use the "Assessment Checklist" (page 90) to evaluate the types of assessments used to formally and informally evaluate learning in the sciences.

Assessment is a complex process that requires aligning subject matter with pedagogy, time, and resources. It is often performed in four stages: diagnostic, formative, summative, and confirmatory (figure 5.1).

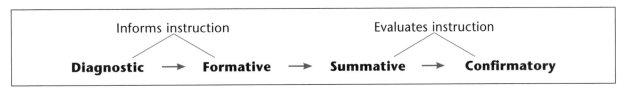

Figure 5.1: Assessment timeline.

Diagnostic Assessment

Diagnostic assessment takes place at the beginning of a new unit of study and provides the teacher with baseline data on what individual students already know and do not know and on the misconceptions they may have about the concepts in the new unit. Diagnostic assessment also establishes an instructional framework for planning or modifying lessons to meet the needs of various students in the class. Because this form of assessment is done at the beginning of a unit, it should not be evaluated for a grade.

Research on diagnostic assessment suggests that it is helpful in informing instruction, because teachers often assume more initial understanding than their students actually have (Sterling, 2002). However, research also suggests that diagnostic assessment instruments that hone in on emerging student understanding are difficult to create, with most initial attempts showing what students do not understand rather than their emerging understanding (Sterling, 2002). For example, if students do poorly on a diagnostic assessment on specific weather topics, it does not mean they are unknowledgeable about weather, because even kindergartners know that it is hot on some days and cold on others. Effective diagnostic assessment hones in on emerging understanding.

Formative Assessment

Formative assessment often takes the form of short assessments that are done throughout the teaching of a unit, preferably daily, in order for the teacher to monitor student progress.

These assessments follow the students' developing understanding of science concepts. Sterling (2002) indicates that (1) multiple short assessments that incorporate several question formats are most effective to determine student understanding of science, (2) teachers are surprised at the numerous misinterpretations and misconceptions that students have even after a science topic has been taught, and (3) both writing about and discussing science concepts aid understanding and enable teachers to follow developing understanding. Be sure that teachers don't just check off that students have completed the assignments. Assignments should be meaningful and gone over in detail. Use walkthroughs, unannounced observations, and a collection of sample assignments with lesson plans to ensure that accountability structures are firmly in place.

Summative Assessment

Summative assessment is usually evaluative and done at the end of the unit for a grade. Research suggests that (1) using multiple forms of assessment is an effective strategy and (2) having students routinely explain why they choose a particular multiple-choice answer requires a deeper level of thinking than just identifying the correct answers (Sterling, 2002).

Confirmatory Assessment

Confirmatory assessment, otherwise known as standardized tests, is usually done by an outside agency to develop an overall picture of how much and what students are learning. State or local school divisions often mandate these tests. Students typically score well on confirmatory tests that ask only multiple-choice questions when classroom instruction routinely includes assessment tasks in which they are required to express their understanding in multiple formats, including explaining their answers on formative or summative multiple-choice classroom tests.

The Integration of Authentic Assessment

Authentic assessments are those that have students perform a real-world task by utilizing acquired knowledge and skills. These tasks should be comparable to problems that adult citizens, consumers, or professionals would face (Wiggins, 1993). Examples could include developing practical strategies to harness sustainable energy to power a city in lieu of nonrenewable resources or to increase the growth rate of produce to sustain a growing human population. Authentic assessments tend to intimidate teachers, because they are different and can necessitate some outside-the-box thinking. However, with some imagination and a few Internet resources, authentic assessments can be a great way for students to apply their knowledge in an engaging and creative way.

Understanding Authentic Assessments

A middle school life-science teacher begins his unit on photosynthesis and plant nutrition with a diagnostic test that asks the students what a plant needs to survive. After collecting and analyzing the diagnostic tests, he sees that all students say sunlight is needed, most say water is needed, and only two say that carbon dioxide is also needed. This indicates to the teacher that the students, for the most part, do not have a sound background in photosynthesis, so he must take his time to make sure that the material is taught to, and absorbed by, the students.

Once the teacher is certain that the students have retained the necessary information, he presents the students with a scenario. The scenario should do the following.

- **Be a problem that would be seen in the real world:** The point of an authentic assessment is to have students solve a problem one would encounter in the course of everyday life or in a field related to what is being taught.

- **Put the students in a specific role:** Give the students a role to take on. Have the students be geologists or botanists or play other roles related to the particular type of problem the students are presented with.

- **Allow the students to apply their knowledge of a topic to the scenario:** Students shouldn't be able to solve this with only the information in the problem. Force students to recall knowledge from what you have just taught and from previous lessons.

- **Do not have one set solution, but rather multiple ways to get a required outcome:** This should not be the kind of problem in which every student reaches the same answer. There should be many ways in which the problem or task can be completed. Allow the students to be creative.

Figure 5.2 shows an example of a performance assessment New Milford School District biology teachers created.

Memo

January 7, 2011

Flowers Galore Corporate Office

Attn: Nursery Managers

The corporate offices of the nursery chain Flowers Galore are asking all nursery managers to find ways to grow bigger, healthier plants more quickly. You are being asked to test different conditions, which cause plants to grow larger, in a shorter amount of time.

You have been given the freedom to test any condition that you would like. You must record all useful data and compare them to plants growing in normal conditions. Nursery managers who contribute useful ideas will be rewarded with a $5,000 bonus.

The CEO has asked that you come up with a presentation for him to see your results. Due to the busy travel schedule of the CEO, he has asked that you put the presentation in the form of an audio or video podcast or a PowerPoint presentation. The CEO will decide whether your information will help the company and ultimately decide if you will receive the $5,000 bonus. The deadline for your presentation will be February 10, 2011.

—Burt Smith, Flowers Galore Nursery Supervisor

Figure 5.2: A real-world performance assessment for a biology class.

This assessment is authentic because it is a real-world problem, involves the students in playing a role, and has many possible solutions. This particular example is completed over the course of a month; however, an authentic assessment could last anywhere from fifteen minutes to an entire grading period.

Grading an authentic assessment should include a rubric so students know what is expected of them. This is vital, particularly at the younger ages when self-direction is not yet as prevalent or established. Showing learners early on what is expected of them will allow them to develop sound foundations that will require less guidance as they move forward in their academic careers.

Assisting Teachers in Assessment of Student Understanding

Diagnostic, formative, and summative assessment informs not only the teacher but also the students of their own understanding or lack of understanding. Assessment that informs students and facilitates their learning should be embedded throughout the instructional process. Teachers should purposefully plan assessment by identifying assessment tasks and criteria and evidence of understanding, as well as modifications for students with special needs. Figure 5.3 is a sample freshman biology assessment rubric based on the nursery example in figure 5.2.

Course: Biology

Name: _____ **Date:** _____

	16–20 Points	10–15 Points	5–9 Points	0–4 Points
Experimental Design	• The question attempting to be answered is clearly stated. • The hypothesis is clearly stated and well thought out, and stated in a way that allows it to be tested. • The procedure is original and described in a way that allows it to be recreated easily. • The manipulated variable, responding variable, and controlled variable are clearly stated.	• The question attempted to be answered is stated and makes sense. • The hypothesis is stated and applicable. • The procedure is listed correctly. • The variables are listed and relevant.	• The question stated is vague and difficult to understand. • The hypothesis is stated but is unclear or unable to be tested. • The procedure does not give a detailed description of the experiment. • The variables are incorrectly labeled.	• The question attempted to be answered is not listed. • The hypothesis is either absent or poorly stated. • The procedure is very poorly stated and does not give the reader the ability to recreate the experiment. • The variables are absent or not stated.
Experimental Design Points				

	16–20 Points	**10–15 Points**	**5–9 Points**	**0–4 Points**
Data	• Data are presented in a clear, well-organized table or chart with proper units. • Data are represented in a properly organized and relevant graph with proper units with a key. • Data are related to the hypothesis, whether to support or disprove it. • All data use proper units. • Data are relevant to the experiment.	• Data are presented in a chart. • Data are also put into a properly labeled graph. • Data are related to the hypothesis. • Most data use proper units. • Nearly all data are relevant to the experiment.	• Data are included in a nonorganized manner. • Data are included in an improperly labeled graph. • Data are only vaguely related to the hypothesis. • Data use wrong or inconsistent units. • Data are largely irrelevant to the experiment.	• Data are absent and sparse. • A graph is absent. • Data are not related to the hypothesis in any way. • Data that are included lack units. • There is no link between data and the hypothesis.
Data Points				
Results	• The results obtained from the experiment were used to properly and accurately support or disprove the hypothesis. • The results are analyzed in an intelligent and accurate manner. • The results are clearly stated in an intelligent, easily understood way. • The conclusion is accurate and well thought out.	• The results obtained from the experiment were used to support or disprove the hypothesis, although not entirely accurate. • The results are sufficiently analyzed. • The results are stated well. • The conclusion is accurate.	• The results obtained from the experiment were only vaguely or inaccurately used to support or disprove the hypothesis. • The results are insufficiently analyzed. • The results are merely stated, not explained. • The conclusion is present but not accurate.	• The results were lacking or completely absent. • The results are not analyzed. • The results are in no way stated to summarize the experiment. • The conclusion is absent.
Results Points				

Figure 5.3: Authentic assessment rubric.

continued →

	16–20 Points	10–15 Points	5–9 Points	0–4 Points
Podcast	• The podcast is informative and presents the results of the experiment in a clear, original way. • The podcast suggests an answer to the CEO that will improve the plants in the nursery. • The podcast meets time criteria.	• The podcast is informative and presents necessary data. • The podcast suggests an answer to the CEO. • The podcast meets time criteria.	• The podcast only vaguely discusses the results of the experiment. • The podcast does not suggest a clear answer to the CEO. • The podcast does not meet time criteria.	• The podcast does not discuss the results of the experiment. • The podcast does not suggest an answer to the CEO at all. • The podcast does not meet time criteria.
Podcast Points				
Experiment	• Learners follow through with the experiment for the duration of the assignment. • Learners pay close attention to the well-being of the plants. • Learners take the time to ensure the experiment is carried out as designed.	• Learners follow through with the experiment for the duration of the assignment. • Learners pay attention to the well-being of the plants. • Learners, for the most part, carry out the experiment as designed.	• Learners follow through with the experiment for most of the assignment. • Learners don't pay as close attention as they should to the well-being of the plants. • Learners stray from the design of their experiment slightly.	• Learners don't follow through with the experiment. • Learners allow the plants to severely wilt or die. • Learners do not conduct the experiment that was planned.
Experiment Points				
Teammate	• Teammates indicated that you went above and beyond in every aspect of the project.	• Teammates indicated that you met all expectations.	• Teammates indicated that you did slightly less than what was expected of you.	• Teammates indicated that you had minimal involvement in the project.
Teammate Points				

In order to obtain data on the status of science assessment and evaluation in your school, survey your teachers. Collect the ideas they generate. Promote discussion about these ideas, and have teachers try them out in their classrooms. Then visit these classrooms and encourage other teachers to do so in order to determine the strategies for assessment and evaluation that work best at specific grade levels. Work as a team with teachers to generate assessment and evaluation guidelines. Use these guidelines to improve science instruction and to evaluate teachers when they are presenting science lessons. The "Survey for Assessment and Evaluation" (page 92) will help get you started.

Assessment Issues

One way to indirectly modify teaching is to have teachers assess student learning. When teachers are able to identify what students do not understand or are struggling with, effective teachers change what or how they teach.

In chapter 3, on evaluating the school's science program (page 31), we suggested using the "Science Program Self-Assessment Survey" (page 77). By simply taking the survey and discussing their answers, teachers will develop a sense of the difference between assessment and evaluation. Assessment includes all processes and tools that focus on learning, while evaluation focuses on grades. The following list provides a variety of assessment techniques to determine the levels of learning that are occurring.

- **Knowledge of when to use which type of assessment:** Recall the assessment timeline in chapter 5 (page 57) showing the relationship among diagnostic, formative, summative, and confirmatory assessment. This graphic organizer can help teachers envision how to embed the assessment process into instruction. After teachers have a conceptual vision of using assessment at different times in the instructional process to inform instruction, they can then use the "Survey for Assessment and Evaluation" (page 92) to guide assessment planning.

- **Effective questions:** To help teachers develop effective test questions, encourage them to analyze state and national test questions. These questions should be analyzed for level (see Bloom's Taxonomy, page 45), question format, and typical responses.

- **Test checklist:** The "Assessment Checklist" (page 90) provides teachers with a tool to analyze their own tests or the tests of others. It helps teachers look at effective assessment planning, questions, answers, and the mechanics of constructing a test.

- **Rubrics:** The purpose of a rubric is to specify the criteria on which a project will be scored. Rubrics can be holistic or analytic. Holistic rubrics provide a score, but not feedback on the project components and concepts that were correct or incorrect. Analytic rubrics, in contrast, provide the student with specific information about what was correct and incorrect and what needs improvement. An example of each is provided in figures 5.4 and 5.5 (page 64).

- **Student work:** When teachers conduct action research on student learning, they do more than construct effective assessment instruments and rubrics. They also analyze what students understand and don't understand and use this information to inform instruction. After grading students' work, teachers need to go back and analyze what students got right and wrong. At this point, they are looking for patterns. Once they identify what the students do not understand, they must decide if it is important enough to reteach. If it is, they develop a plan to help students clarify their understanding. In general, teachers are looking for what works, what doesn't, and how to improve it.

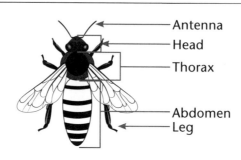

Excellent
The insect body has a head, abdomen, and thorax. The body parts are proportional to the size of the insect. The insect has six jointed legs that are correctly positioned in the body. Optional wings, mouthparts, and so on are correct in size and located in the correct place. The student is able to name each body part correctly.

Satisfactory
The insect has a head, abdomen, and thorax. The insect has six legs that are correctly positioned. The student can name the main body parts.

Needs Improvement
The insect is missing a main body part. The six legs are not in the correct position. The student cannot name all the main body parts.

Figure 5.4: Sample holistic rubric for assessment on insects.

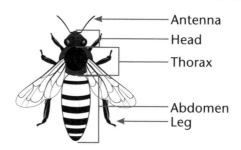

Characteristics
Body: Head, abdomen, and thorax
Proportion
Legs
Wings, mouthparts, and so on
Labels

Needs Improvement
Only one part of the insect identified
Very incorrect proportion
Six legs not correctly positioned in the body
Not correct size and not correct placement
Main body parts not named correctly

Satisfactory
Two parts identified
Slightly incorrect proportion
Six legs correctly positioned in the body
Correct size or correct placement
Main body parts named correctly

Excellent
Three parts identified
Correct proportion
Six jointed legs correctly positioned in the body
Correct size and correct placement
Each body part named correctly

Figure 5.5: Sample analytic rubric for assessment on insects.

Most teachers need help in planning effective assessment instruments. These strategies provide teachers with experiences that will enable them to construct more effective assessments, which can then be used to inform instruction.

Summary

Assessments can take many shapes and forms and can be used for an assortment of purposes. However, at the core of all assessments is the goal of monitoring student learning and growth. Familiarizing yourself with each type of assessment and communicating information to your staff are essential in making sure your teachers are effectively gauging student comprehension. Being able to assess students in a variety of ways, and to effectively analyze the data these assessments produce, will only make your teachers more effective in their practices.

SIX
PROFESSIONAL DEVELOPMENT

For standards-based reform to work in science teaching and learning, teacher professional development needs to be sustainable, comprehensive, collaborative, and inquiry based. If possible, it should be embedded into the instructional day. It also needs to include a review of science concepts, particularly in the area of STEM, as well as methods to guide and assess student learning. Furthermore, it needs to address teachers' fears and concerns about finding time to teach science and about their knowledge of the subject matter.

A main goal of professional development in science education is to strengthen teachers' ability to design and teach effective, hands-on, inquiry-based lessons and create assessments that are authentic and multilayered. Since many teachers have never been exposed to scientific inquiry experiences, having them participate as learners in inquiry-based science provides them with the opportunity to understand learning from this perspective. In addition, the experience provides them with the opportunity to analyze their feelings as learners, discuss challenges from a teacher's perspective, and increase their subject-matter knowledge. When modeling science teaching during staff development sessions, facilitators must continually pose the questions: What are we doing as teachers? Why?

Traditional professional development involves teachers sitting in a seminar, listening to a lecture, and taking the knowledge they are just given to do with as they please. With teachers working together as a community, more discussion and sharing take place, with added accountability on each of the community members, because teachers are working toward a common goal: increasing student achievement. This view of professional development is known as a teacher team. According to the NRC (2007), having teachers collaborate with one another to reach a common goal is important:

> When teacher teams, work groups, and departments function as communities of practice, numerous studies have shown strong, desirable effects on faculty

willingness to implement instructional reforms, teacher relationships with students, and student achievement outcomes. (p. 308)

> **Principles of Quality Professional Development**
>
> Using knowledge from research, theory, and the wisdom of experienced, practicing professional developers, we suggest five principles of effective professional development. They are the following.
>
> 1. **Keep students and their learning at the core, and that means all students:** Science education reforms—and the national, state, and local standards on which they are based—share a common commitment to high standards of achievement for all students and not just the few who are talented or privileged. This implies a different perspective on the content students should learn and the teaching strategies teachers should use. To meet this challenge, all professional development resources, including teacher time, must be focused on rigorous content and the best ways to reach all students.
>
> 2. **Use a rich knowledge base and develop it through professional learning experiences:** Pedagogical content knowledge (Shulman, 1987) involves knowing how to teach specific science concepts and principles to young people at different developmental levels. This kind of knowledge and skill is unique to teaching and distinguishes what teachers know from what scientists know. Knowledge of science content, although critical, is not enough, just as knowledge of general pedagogy is not enough. The goal of developing pedagogical content knowledge must be the focus of professional development opportunities for teachers.
>
> 3. **Use principles that guide the improvement of student learning to guide professional learning for teachers and other educators:** Professional developers must *walk the talk* because people tend to teach in ways in which they have learned. Engaging in active learning, focusing on fewer ideas more deeply, and learning collaboratively are all principles that must characterize learning for teachers if they, in turn, will apply these to helping their students learn.
>
> 4. **Draw from both research and practice:** Professional development opportunities must honor the knowledge of the practicing teacher as well as draw on research and other sources of expertise outside schools and classrooms. Artful professional development design effectively combines theory and practice.
>
> 5. **Align with and support system-based changes that promote student learning:** Professional development has long suffered because of its separation from other critical elements of the education system, with the result that new ideas and strategies are not implemented. Although professional development is not a panacea, it can support changes in such areas as standards, assessment, and curriculum, creating the culture and capacity for continuous improvement that is so critical for educators facing current and future challenges.
>
> *Source: Loucks-Horsley, Hewson, Love, & Stiles 1998.*

Planning a Meaningful Professional Development Program

At the most basic level, the principal guides professional development by having teachers set goals, plan, do, and reflect. Professional development isn't only attending training; it is becoming involved.

Productivity in a teacher team increases when teachers work together. That being said, groups of teachers should be allowed to choose topics that, in their opinion, will increase student achievement. This will often be far more valuable than going to a standard professional development seminar, as it will allow the teacher teams to work together and research best practices in an area about which they are passionate. As the principal, it is your job to offer guidance, suggest ideas, and set guidelines for the learning community to accomplish its goals. With regard to science, you need to assess your teachers' strengths and weaknesses and work from there.

To ensure accountability, teachers who are working in their respective teams should keep minutes of each meeting and set goals. The principal should review the goals and the minutes to ensure that these meetings are productive. In addition, the goals that are set should be measurable using hard data. This will provide feedback to both the teacher team and the principal on whether their efforts are having a positive effect.

The keys to arranging a successful teacher team are (Hord, 2009):

- Shared beliefs, values, and vision of what the school should be
- Shared and supportive leadership where power, authority, and decision making are distributed across the community
- Supportive structural conditions, such as time, place, and resources
- Supportive relational conditions that include respect and caring among the community, with trust as an imperative
- Collective learning, intentionally determined, to address student needs and the increased effectiveness of the professionals
- Peers sharing their practice to gain feedback, and thus individual and organizational improvement

The Process of Professional Development

Many strategies can be used to facilitate the professional development process and foster continuous improvement. A teacher team can take infinite shapes and forms as it progresses through time. Support teachers in forming their own teams on the first day of school to brainstorm what they would like to research over the course of the year. Allow the groups to research topics that would be helpful to their particular needs; for example, science teachers may want to research the effectiveness of inquiry-based lessons on student retention of material versus the effectiveness of traditional methods. This will allow teachers to explore this topic and motivate them to implement such practices in their everyday teaching. It also gives them the freedom to guide their own professional development. You may want to approve each team's topic to ensure that it is appropriate for its disciplines.

The team should monitor its efforts. Giving individual groups the freedom to run their own meetings will convey your trust in the staff and motivate them to work hard. All Things PLC (www.allthingsplc.info) contains a wealth of information to assist you in the process of establishing your teacher teams and overall professional development goals.

Teacher teams are a far more effective way to allow your teachers to control their own professional development. Allowing teams to select their own topics and seminars to attend will allow them to take ownership of their professional development initiatives. Some additional ways teachers can enrich their professional development include the following.

- **Completing the interview on science connections:** Have teachers complete the "Reflective Discussion Guidelines" reproducible (page 79). This will help them assess if they are having difficulty with science content knowledge.

- **Participating as a learner:** In order for teachers to teach inquiry-based science, they must understand what it is. Many teachers find it easier to teach inquiry-based science once they have participated in instruction themselves as a learner. Therefore, all subject-matter professional development should have teachers performing experiments and learning science through hands-on, inquiry-based methods. This allows them to see this approach modeled and to participate as learners.

- **Analyzing video recordings:** Looking at different approaches to teaching can be informative and helps teachers focus on the key issues of effective teaching. The *Trends in International Mathematics and Science Study* (NCES, 1999; http://nces.ed.gov/timss/video.asp) has produced an excellent series of videos profiling teachers from the United States, Japan, and Germany. Annenberg Learner (1997; www.learner.org/resources/series21.html) has a fantastic video library for K–8 science teachers that analyzes case studies in science education.

- **Recording themselves:** It can be an eye-opening experience for teachers to view video recordings of themselves teaching. These recordings do not have to be shared with others. However, having a critical friend with whom a teacher can share his or her recordings can enhance learning. Additionally, sharing short video clips of what worked and what didn't with teacher commentary on how to improve the lesson is a sign that you are establishing a school that values continuous improvement.

- **Observing others:** Teachers can benefit greatly from observing one another. For example, if students are having difficulty learning a concept, the teacher might observe another teacher who is teaching this same topic to see how he or she is presenting the material. For this to work, however, teachers must understand that the observation is not evaluative and that only positive feedback should be given—unless the observed teacher asks for constructive feedback.

Professional Development Program Evaluation

Evaluating the success of professional development efforts takes time and is the key to ongoing improvement. These evaluations should not be an afterthought but must be thoroughly planned in conjunction with the planning of the program. The reproducible "Tracking the Impact of Professional Development" (page 93) has sample questions, activities, and online resources to assist you in evaluating your staff development program.

There are a variety of opportunities for teachers to engage in professional development related to the sciences. Many of these cannot count toward requirements for license renewal or professional development hours, because they are not carefully documented. Consider using the tracking form over the course of the year to record the impact that science-related professional development is having on instruction, curriculum, STEM connections, lab development, and technology integration.

Barriers to Professional Development

If your school system does not offer professional development courses for science, then you may want to make funds available for teachers to travel to state or national science teacher conferences. Your PTA may be another possible source of funding to send teachers from your school to these conferences, or the PTA may support the purchase of science equipment for your school. Another possibility is to combine funds with other elementary or middle schools in your district or county to hire a science consultant to provide in-service training for your staff. Local colleges and universities often serve as a source for finding consultants. Also, most colleges and universities offer courses for elementary and middle school teachers to improve science content knowledge and pedagogy. Another possibility is to use the Internet to access on-demand webinars relating to science instruction and the incorporation of STEM activities, such as those offered by *Education Week* (www.edweek.org) and the Teacher Learning Community (http://simplek12.com/tlc/webinars).

Summary

The principal needs to be a leader, observer, coach, mentor, supporter, and guide in the professional development process. Effective professional development is long term, with a series of related short-term plans. With your faculty, collaboratively choose a focus for the year, and plan all professional development to support and extend that focus. Teachers need time to be exposed to new ideas, try them out, and report back on what works and does not work.

APPENDIX A
REPRODUCIBLES

The following reproducibles will greatly assist you as you move toward enhancing your school's overall science program. They will serve as guides and foundational elements to improve instruction, evaluate curricular materials, comprehensively assess the program, and analyze the impact of professional development initiatives.

Evaluating Science Curricular Materials

Name of evaluator: _____ Date: _____

Resource being evaluated: _____ Score: _____

This tool is designed to assist school administrators to collect information from teachers, parents, and other interested stakeholders on possible new science curricular materials. For each of the following statements, please indicate (1) the extent to which you think the new resource meets each criterion—not at all, somewhat, or definitely—and (2) the level at which current curricular materials that the school already possesses meet each criterion—rarely, somewhat, or mostly—by circling one of the three numbers on the right-hand side. Resources that receive the highest scores should be considered for adoption.

Please circle your role in our school community: Teacher   Parent   Other _____

	Does the resource meet the specified criterion?			Is the criterion emphasized in current curricular materials?		
	Not at All	Somewhat	Definitely	Rarely	Somewhat	Mostly
1. Provides a sense of purpose as to the importance of learning scientific concepts, phenomena, and events	1	2	3	1	2	3
2. Takes into account student ideas	1	2	3	1	2	3
3. Incorporates STEM principles	1	2	3	1	2	3
4. Engages students with relevant phenomena to foster excitement and a general interest	1	2	3	1	2	3
5. Contains an array of hands-on, inquiry-based learning activities	1	2	3	1	2	3
6. Promotes problem solving and critical thinking on scientific concepts	1	2	3	1	2	3

	Does the resource meet the specified criterion?			Is the criterion emphasized in current curricular materials?		
	Not at All	Somewhat	Definitely	Rarely	Somewhat	Mostly
7. Assesses student progress through a variety of differentiated assessments to determine learning of students with different needs	1	2	3	1	2	3
8. Enhances the science learning environment	1	2	3	1	2	3
9. Provides a web-based component to facilitate learning both inside and outside of the classroom	1	2	3	1	2	3
10. Infuses connections to other major content areas (math, history, language arts, physical education or health, or the arts)	1	2	3	1	2	3

Experimental Design Diagram

Title: The effect _____ on _____

Hypothesis: If _____ is _____

then _____ will _____

Independent variable:

Levels:

Trials:

Dependent variable:

Constants:

Source: Adapted from Cothron, Giese, & Rezba, 2000.

Science Program Self-Assessment Survey

Name:

School:

The survey is divided into five main categories: science program content, assessment, teacher preparedness, school climate, and school system support. Read the question in each section and rate them 1–5 according to the following scale:

1 = Poor, nonexistent, or never
2 = Low, rarely, or sometimes
3 = Medium, average, or half the time
4 = Above average, usually, or most of the time
5 = Excellent, continually, or almost all the time

Add your scores for all the surveys and then read the scenario that corresponds to your total score on pp. 33–36 of *What Principals Need to Know About Teaching and Learning Science*.

Science Program Content	Score 1–5
Does your school have a science program that lists overall goals, grade-level benchmarks, and individual behavior indicators for each course and grade?	
Does each grade level have a list of print materials, textbooks, library books, and supplemental activity sheets to support science instruction?	
Does each grade have a list of computer software, videos, DVDs, and so on that support science instruction?	
Does each grade level have a list of current websites that support science instruction?	
Does your school have a science laboratory or designated science area in the building to support and extend science instruction?	
Do you have a teacher who is highly qualified in science, or do you have training in the sciences for teachers?	
Does the curriculum address STEM initiatives and the importance of interdisciplinary connections?	
Total	

Assessment	Score 1–5
Does each grade level have assessments correlated to benchmarks and indicators in the science program to determine what students know and are able to do at a given time? Does each grade level have hands-on authentic assessments and evaluations correlated to benchmarks and indicators in the science program to determine what students know and are able to do at a given time?	
Do teachers do preassessment activities at the start of each major science unit to allow them to differentiate instruction as they teach the unit?	
Do teachers give a separate grade for science homework and class effort and another grade for knowledge of content?	
Do teachers provide grading rubrics at the start of assignments so everyone (teacher, students, administrators, and parents or guardians) understands what is being emphasized and what needs to be done to attain various grades on projects, homework, and tests?	
Total	

Teacher Preparedness	Score 1–5
Does each classroom teacher attend professional development programs to learn the science content, research-based instructional strategies, and classroom-management techniques needed to effectively teach his or her grade-level science content?	
Does each classroom teacher have a list of all support materials required to teach the science program for his or her grade level?	
Does each classroom teacher have a list of all support materials required to teach the science program for his or her grade level?	
Do grade-level teams have adequate planning time to prepare science lessons and learning activities?	
Does your school have a mentor program to support new teachers or teachers new to the grade level with planning and implementing science instruction?	
Do classroom teachers implement a variety of teaching strategies—whole group, small group, individual instruction, student-centered, hands-on, demonstration, lecture, and multimedia—when teaching science?	
Total	

School Climate	Score 1–5
Is there evidence throughout the school—grounds, hallways, cafeteria, media center, gym, and classrooms—that science is taught and science knowledge is valued? Are there school events focusing on science, such as Science Discovery Night, Invention Convention, Family Science Night, Science Week, or worldwide awareness days like National Wildlife Week or Earth Day?	
Are field trips associated with science content regularly planned for each grade level?	
Are teachers and school volunteers recognized for outstanding achievements in science education?	
Does your community recognize that your science program is meeting the needs of all students who attend your school?	
Total	

School System Support	Score 1–5
Does your school system have a science curriculum supervisor or central staff administrator responsible for coordinating science instruction?	
Does your school support participation in local, state, and national science competitions like Science Olympiad, National Science Bowl, and National Science Decathlon?	
Does your school system have specific annual goals for improving science instruction?	
Does your school system provide the monetary support to implement the current science program and integrate technology?	
Does your school system provide opportunities for staff development to properly instruct the current science program?	
Do other school systems in your region or state recognize your school system as a leader in providing quality science education?	
Total	
Grand total	

Reflective Discussion Guidelines

When you engage a teacher in a reflective discussion after observing a lesson, the teacher should be able to easily describe the science connections between what was taught on a particular day and the entire unit. The emphasis here is on *discussion*: postobservation meetings should be open and honest conversations about behaviors and pedagogical techniques seen in the lesson. The discussion should serve as a catalyst for reflection on the part of the teacher in order to improve classroom instruction. Use this time as an opportunity to get the teacher's perspective. (Write the unit and lesson topics as essential questions.)

Unit Topic	
Length of Unit	
Standards Addressed During Unit	
Lesson Topic	
Length of Lesson (Time Frames for Each Component)	
Standards Addressed During Lesson	

Use the following questions to stimulate an open dialogue with the teacher about science teaching practices.

1. What is the objective of today's lesson?

2. How does this build on prior knowledge from previous science lessons?

3. How will you build on it during the next science lesson?

4. How did you incorporate STEM concepts and 21st century skills?

5. How did you effectively integrate technology?

6. How do the science concepts taught today connect and support the science being taught in the unit?

7. What science concepts did the students learn from today's lesson? How do you know?

8. What science concepts do the students need more work on? How do you know?

Planning to Teach for Understanding I

Planning team members: _____

Grade level: _____

Subject: _____

Length of unit: _____

Curriculum topic or theme: _____

Standards: _____
_____

Brainstorm a list of what students should know and be able to do on this topic or theme.

Planning to Teach for Understanding II

Planning team members: _____

Grade level: _____

Subject: _____

Length of unit: _____

Curriculum topic or theme: _____

Standards: _____
_____

Understanding: Categorize what students will know and be able to do.

Questions: Phrase the key content to be taught in the form of questions.

Evidence of understanding: Determine how students will demonstrate their essential understanding.

Essential understanding: List three to five key concepts or skills.

Important knowledge: Include information that connects concepts and disciplines.

Worth knowing: Brainstorm information that is usually not formally assessed on a quiz or test.

Direct Observation Inventory

Date: _____ Time: _____

Directions: In less than five minutes, observe the types of activities that are taking place during science instruction.

Note: This inventory does not assess the quality of instruction, only the type of instruction that is taking place.

Discussion

What type of discussion is it?

- ☐ Teacher-led
- ☐ Student-led
- ☐ Lab experiment

Teacher

What types of verbal cues is the teacher giving?

- ☐ Laboratory directions
- ☐ Science information
- ☐ General directions

Students

How are students working and learning?

- ☐ Individual
- ☐ Small group
- ☐ Whole class
- ☐ Leading the discussion
- ☐ On the side (doing lab activities, demonstrations, differentiated activities)
- ☐ Other: _____

What types of hands-on activities are students engaged in?

- ☐ Real science equipment
- ☐ Pseudo-science equipment
- ☐ Data analysis

- ☐ Mathematical data analysis
- ☐ Qualitative data analysis

How are students participating?

- ☐ Reading books, newspapers, articles, or something similar
- ☐ Laboratory experiments
- ☐ Textbook work
- ☐ Student-centered activities (such as cooperative learning, projects)
- ☐ Other: _____

How are students using technology?

- ☐ Internet
- ☐ Simulations
- ☐ Searching
- ☐ Word processors
- ☐ Data analysis
- ☐ Digital media
- ☐ Nonscience work

Indicators of Ineffective Science Instruction

Rate the following examples of ineffective K–8 science instruction.

	Not Evident	Partially Evident	Clearly Evident
Climate			
Nonexistent or limited STEM connections			
Not enough materials for each student to be fully engaged			
Teacher demonstrations of what students should do			
No science equipment and materials in sight			
No connections to real-world applications			
Hands-on but not minds-on			
Worksheets that don't organize hands-on investigations and concept development			
"Cookbook" laboratory activities (cookbook labs are better than no labs)			
No science role models			
No evidence of technology integration			
Discussion and Questions			
More teacher talk than student talk			
Discussion only of procedures and not underlying science concepts			
No summary discussions that facilitate concept development and connections			
Low-level, fact-oriented teacher questions			
One-word student or teacher responses			
Passive learners			
No student questions			
Lack of wait time when students ask or respond to questions			
Language Arts			
Reading the text and answering the questions at the end of the section			
Unfocused reading to cover the material—for example, reading the entire chapter			
Language arts strategies applied to science in lieu of doing science			
Focus on long list of definitions especially at the beginning of the unit (vocabulary should be introduced in context after the students have had time to explore)			
Science word puzzles			

Observation Guidelines for K–8 Science Classroom Learning Climate

Rate the following examples of K–8 science classroom learning climate.

	Not Evident	Partially Evident	Clearly Evident
Classroom organized and arranged for hands-on, inquiry-based science			
Students learning science through investigation and inquiry			
A focus on the scientific processes			
Active involvement in learning			
Adaptations to meet individual student strengths and needs			
Students working productively in small groups			
Students moving around to accomplish tasks			
Productive student chatter			
Supportive classroom community			
Teachers moving among groups to engage students in discussing science			
Teachers facilitating students in drawing accurate conclusions based on evidence			

Observation Guidelines for K–8 Science Teachers

Rate the following examples of K–8 science teaching.

	Not Evident	Partially Evident	Clearly Evident
Organizing materials and equipment before students arrive			
Establishing routines			
Assigning student responsibility for the care of materials and equipment			
Ensuring a safe learning environment			
Activating prior science knowledge through questioning and discussion			
Presenting the question or problem that drives the lesson			
Connecting classroom science with science and scientists in the real world			
Modeling and demonstrating science concepts and procedures			
Using questioning techniques to assist students in making connections among concepts			
Actively observing, recording, and assessing students' responses and participation			
Assisting students in drawing conclusions and forming generalizations			
Providing appropriate follow-up activities			

Source: Adapted from Fairfax County Public Schools, Virginia.

Observation Guidelines for K–8 Science Students

Rate the following examples of K–8 science learning.

	Not Evident	Partially Evident	Clearly Evident
Using hands-on science materials and equipment			
Using science materials in ways similar to scientists			
Using experimental designs by:			
• Exhibiting and using background knowledge			
• Identifying problems and asking questions			
• Raising meaningful concerns			
• Researching a hypothesis			
• Designing an experiment			
• Conducting experiments systematically			
• Making insightful observations			
• Recording and classifying data on charts, graphs, and logs			
• Analyzing data			
• Expressing findings mathematically or scientifically			
• Formulating explanations from evidence			
• Drawing conclusions			
• Forming generalizations			
• Sharing observations			
• Working cooperatively in groups			
• Using and maintaining science equipment responsibly			
• Sharing results by informally sharing, giving presentations, writing reports, using displays, and using graphics			
Defending and justifying explanations			

Source: Adapted from Fairfax County Public Schools, Virginia.

Observation Guidelines for K–8 Science Classroom Environment

Rate the following examples of an effective K–8 teaching environment.

	Not Evident	Partially Evident	Clearly Evident
Hands-on science equipment and materials set up to use			
Science-exploration centers			
Student science work, projects, and models			
Bulletin-board displays, charts, posters, and diagrams			
Science trade books and resource materials			
Science-conducive workspace, tables and counters, windows, sinks with running water			
Technology—Probeware, computers and software, Internet access			

Source: Adapted from Fairfax County Public Schools, Virginia.

Observation Guidelines for K–8 Schoolwide Science Climate

Rate the following examples of an effective K–8 schoolwide science climate.

	Not Evident	Partially Evident	Clearly Evident
Signs of science in the building entrance and on the marquee			
Hall bulletin boards displaying student science work			
Science focus areas such as gardens, labs, and pond			
Public address announcements about science information			
Family science events and parental involvement			
Business and community partnerships for science			
Field trips to science sites or virtual trips			
Staff development that focuses on science concept development and real-world applications			
Staff with an interest in science			
Principal actively promoting science learning			

Source: Adapted from Fairfax County Public Schools, Virginia.

Assessment Checklist

Planning

- ☐ Standards and critical understanding were identified before assessment was created.
- ☐ The assessment instrument assesses the identified standards.
- ☐ Each item on the assessment can be linked to at least one standard.
- ☐ The assessment instrument was created before the subject matter was taught.
- ☐ A grading scale for the assessment was determined before the subject matter was taught.
- ☐ There is a scoring guide and answer key for the assessment.
- ☐ For students that finish early, I plan to have them _____.

Mechanics

- ☐ There is a specific place for the students to write their names.
- ☐ Point value is given for each section of the assessment.
- ☐ There is enough open space on the assessment to give it a student-friendly appearance.
- ☐ The assessment instrument is not so long that it uses unnecessary resources (like too much paper or ink).
- ☐ There is enough room for the students to answer to each question.
- ☐ The assessment instrument looks professional.

Questions

- ☐ There are _____ (number) formats of questions on the assessment instrument, which are _____.
- ☐ The tasks on the assessment address the following _____ (number) multiple intelligences: _____.
- ☐ There are _____ (number) levels of Bloom's Taxonomy on the assessment instrument, which are _____.
- ☐ There are _____ (number) higher-order-thinking questions on the assessment, which are _____.
- ☐ The questions cover all essential understanding for the topic.
- ☐ The assessment is adapted to students with special needs by _____.

- ☐ Providing students with a choice of questions to answer was considered.
- ☐ For open-ended questions, there are criteria to guide students in answering questions.

Answers

- ☐ There is only one correct answer to each closed-ended question.
- ☐ All incorrect answer choices for closed-ended questions are plausible distractors.
- ☐ All answer choices for closed-ended questions are approximately the same length.

Survey for Assessment and Evaluation

Work as a team with teachers to generate assessment and evaluation guidelines to improve science instruction and to evaluate teachers when they are presenting science lessons. Ask teachers the following questions to ensure that all students are understanding, applying, and learning the concepts.

1. Do you plan the method of evaluation you will use at the start of developing lesson plans for a new unit? Please provide a brief example.

2. What instructional techniques do you use to ensure the students are aware of each science unit's objectives and the focus of the day's lesson? Please describe them.

3. Do you develop rubrics to assess student projects and assignments? If so, provide a brief example.

4. List the best methods you use on a routine basis for assessing whether a student has mastered a skill or understood a concept. Provide an example.

5. How do you notify students about the type of assessment you will use to determine understanding and to evaluate for a grade?

6. How do you modify instruction and what action do you take to assess your class and determine that approximately 20 percent are not ready to be evaluated on a particular unit that was just covered? Provide an example.

7. What differentiated methods do you use to evaluate students?

8. How do you provide feedback to students about test results and the clarification of misconceptions that may persist regarding certain science concepts?

What Principals Need to Know About Teaching and Learning Science © 2013 Solution Tree Press • solution-tree.com
Visit **go.solution-tree.com/leadership** to download this page.

Tracking the Impact of Professional Development

Title of activity: _____

(If this activity was not a formal experience with a defined title, generate a generic title that can be used to refer to this activity in our conversations about your professional growth.)

General Information

Type of Activity

- ☐ Video conference
- ☐ Online course
- ☐ Workshop
- ☐ Conference
- ☐ Social media interaction
- ☐ Webinar
- ☐ Book or article
- ☐ Blog reading, writing, or commenting
- ☐ Other: _____

Date of activity: _____

(If this activity is a part of a longer conversation, include a starting and ending date for your work.)

Time invested: _____

(Please estimate the amount of time that you've invested in this activity and any follow-up work done as a result of new ideas that you've learned. Be prepared to justify your estimate when asked.)

Links to Online Evidence of Your Participation in This Activity

(This can include links to Twitter messages or posts in digital forums. It can also include links to comments left on—or entries written for—blogs. Remember to use link shorteners like http://bit.ly or http://snipurl.com to make sharing links to online evidence manageable.)

Questions to Consider

1. Briefly describe the nature of this professional learning experience.

2. How did this learning experience connect to our school's mission and vision statements?

3. How did this learning experience connect to your own personal growth plans? Why was this learning experience important to you as an educator? How will it change who you are as a science teacher?

4. How will you integrate what you have been learning into your science instruction?

5. How do you intend to build on this learning experience? Will there be additional studies involved? Are you planning new lessons as a result of what you've learned? Can you share what you've learned with other teachers on our faculty?

APPENDIX B
RESOURCES FOR LEARNING MORE

Throughout *What Principals Need to Know About Teaching and Learning Science*, we've presented various strategies and ideas to assist your school in developing, sustaining, and constantly improving your overall science program. The following resources will provide principals with specific information that can be referenced or integrated immediately to begin the process of creating a more relevant, meaningful, interdisciplinary, and rigorous program.

Elementary School Resources

Chapter 2 introduced a variety of science kits that could be integrated into the curriculum and instruction. The following list provides specific details on kits appropriate for the elementary level and websites to discover more information.

Activities Integrating Mathematics and Science (AIMS)

www.aimsedu.org

AIMS is a collection of teacher books with integrated mathematics and science activities for grades K–9.

Full Option Science System (FOSS)

http://lhsfoss.org, www.fossweb.com

FOSS is a kit-based elementary school science program designed to provide meaningful science education for all students in diverse classrooms and to prepare them for life in the 21st century. FOSS incorporates methodologies such as hands-on inquiry and interdisciplinary projects with contemporary methodologies such as multisensory observation and collaborative learning groups.

Great Explorations in Math and Science (GEMS)

http://lhsgems.org

GEMS is a supplemental enrichment program for students from preschool through eighth grade. There are over seventy inquiry-based teachers' guides.

Insights

http://cse.edc.org/curriculum/insightsElem

Insights is a hands-on, inquiry-based elementary school science curriculum. The seventeen modules reflect a balance of life, physical, and earth sciences.

Science and Technology Concepts™ (STC)

www.carolinacurriculum.com/STC/index.asp

STC is a kit-based, hands-on science program for students grades K–10. The STC program has four modules for each grade level that are designed to develop critical-thinking and problem-solving skills and provide all students with experiences in the life, earth, and physical sciences with technology.

Middle School Resources

Chapter 2 introduced a variety of science kits that could be integrated into the curriculum and instruction. The following list provides specific details on kits appropriate for the middle level and websites to discover more information.

Foundational Approaches in Science Teaching (FAST)

http://manoa.hawaii.edu/crdg/curriculum-materials

FAST is a sequence of three textbooks for middle school: FAST 1–The Local Environment; FAST 2–Matter and Energy in the Biosphere; and FAST 3–Change Over Time.

Full Option Science System (FOSS)

http://lhsfoss.org, www.fossweb.com

FOSS has developed a middle school program of nine courses in three strands: life science, physical science and technology, and earth and space science. The middle school courses carry on the FOSS philosophy by using direct personal experience and inquiry as the starting point of investigations and employing the strategies of collaboration and discourse to help students turn data and information into understanding.

Science and Technology Concepts for Middle Schools™ (STC/MS)

www.stcms.si.edu/stcms.htm

STC/MS is a kit-based, inquiry-centered middle school science curriculum developed for the middle grades. Each of the eight STC/MS modules provides firsthand experiences with scientific phenomena for students.

Science Fusion

www.hmheducation.com//sciencefusion

Science Fusion is a comprehensive, digitally focused curriculum solution that provides all the tools K–8 teachers need to engage students in exciting, inquiry-based learning at every point of instruction. A complete lab program provides hands-on and virtual lab experiences that complement core print and digital paths.

Technology Resources

Technology plays a huge role in the lives of students outside of school and can be used to increase engagement, promote inquiry, and assist with mastering scientific concepts. The following resources will provide you with the foundation to effectively integrate a variety of technology resources into the curriculum for teachers.

- **Probeware:** Probeware is educational software or hardware that is utilized to collect real-time data (such as temperature, salinity, and pH) that can then be displayed on a calculator or computer. Consider the following websites:
    - Vernier (www.vernier.com)
    - Texas Instruments (www.ti.com)
    - Nova (http://fourieredu.com)
    - Really Easy Data Collectors (www.reallyeasydata.com)
    - Pasco (www.pasco.com)
- **Simulations:** Science simulations are used to display phenomena and concepts that are often difficult to visualize and work to develop conceptual understanding. Consider the following websites:
    - PhET (http://phet.colorado.edu)
    - Houghton Mifflin Science (www.eduplace.com/kids/hmsc/content/simulation)
    - ExploreLearning (www.explorelearning.com)
    - NASA Online (www.knowitall.org/nasa/simulations/science.html)
    - BrainPOP (www.brainpop.com)
    - Exploratorium (www.exploratorium.edu)
    - Online Labs (http://onlinelabs.in)

Educational Resources

The following list provides a wealth of information on science resources including tips for effectively integrating various technologies, lesson plans, teaching research, case studies, and strategies to infuse STEM.

- **The Access Center (www.k8accesscenter.org/training_resources/sci_tech_resources .asp):** The Access Center provides a wealth of K–8 teaching and learning resources. The site summarizes each resource by grade level, content area, type, and URL.

- **American Association for the Advancement of Science Project 2061 (www .project2061.org):** The purpose of Project 2061 is to increase science literacy. This resource provides valuable print and online tools.

- **Association for Science Education (ASE; www.ase.org.uk):** A dynamic community of science educators based in the United Kingdom. This website provides numerous innovative resources.

- **Association for Science Teacher Education (ASTE; http://theaste.org):** ASTE promotes the professional development of science teachers across the globe. It is a leader in providing information in the areas of research and policy development aimed at enhancing science teaching.

- **Association for Supervision and Curriculum Development (ASCD; www.ascd.org):** ASCD is an educational leadership organization focused on providing professional development, leadership, and capacity solutions to improve teaching and learning.

- **Birmingham Grid for Learning (www.bgfl.org/bgfl/15.cfm?s=15&p=249,index):** The Birmingham Grid for Learning is a comprehensive portal for interactive educational content. The website provides interactive science whiteboard activities.

- **Case Studies in Science Education (www.learner.org/resources/series21.html):** These short video programs highlight innovative K–8 science teachers and their techniques to improve science instruction and achievement.

- **Eisenhower National Clearinghouse for Mathematics and Science Education (www .goenc.com):** This website offers science teachers access to more than 27,000 multimedia, print, and professional development resources.

- **Elementary Interactive Smartboard Sites (www.sachem.edu/dept/sd/smartboard /elementary%20resources.htm):** Hosted from Sachem, one of the largest school districts in New York, this website includes whiteboard activities perfect for elementary science.

- **Federal Resources for Educational Excellence (www.free.ed.gov):** The U.S. Department of Education offers science teaching and learning resources from federal agencies.

- **getSTEM (www.getstem-mn.com):** This website focuses on STEM news, events, successes, links, media, and forums.

- **International Society for Technology in Education (ISTE; www.iste.org):** ISTE is a global organization committed to improving teaching and learning through the effective use and integration of technology.

- **Middle School Science (www.middleschoolscience.com):** This middle school science site has a searchable database of lesson plans, activities, and ideas.

- **NASA Education (www.nasa.gov/offices/education/about/index.html):** This is the official site for NASA's education initiatives. It provides a wealth of information on specific programs for teachers, education contacts, the NASA Kids' Club, and articles and teaching materials for educators.

- **National Association for Research in Science Teaching (NARST; www.narst.org):** NARST promotes research in science education and disseminates it to improve teaching and learning. It also publishes the *Journal of Research in Science Teaching*.

- **National Science Teachers Association (NSTA; www.nsta.org):** NSTA is an organization committed to promoting innovation and excellence in science teaching at all levels. The website provides an extensive collection of information about the teaching of science.

- **Partnership for 21st Century Skills (P21; www.p21.org):** The mission of P21 is to increase 21st century readiness by fusing critical thinking, problem solving, communication, collaboration, and creativity and innovation. The website has tools and resources, state initiatives, and events and news to improve their science program.

- **PBS Teachers STEM Education Resource Center (www.pbs.org/teachers/stem):** This PBS site provides video and other forms of online content with a focus on STEM. The website breaks resources down to each STEM category and also provides webinars and ideas for professional development.

- **Promethean Planet (www.prometheanplanet.com/en-us/resources/subjects/science):** This is the world's largest interactive whiteboard community. Science resources are broken down by theme and publisher-created resources. There are also teacher features and science teachers' lounge sections.

- **Science Education Journals (www.csun.edu/science/ref/professional_development/sci_ed_journals.html):** This is a comprehensive listing of science journals broken down into specific categories.

- **Science Internet Resource Links (www.delicious.com/Esheninger/science_resources):** This Delicious stack provides some of the best science Internet resources, with each link containing a description of the resource.

- **SMART Exchange (http://exchange.smarttech.com/search.html?subject=Science):** This SMART Technologies site includes a comprehensive listing of science activities and standards-correlated lessons to integrate interactive whiteboards.

- **STEM Education Coalition (www.stemedcoalition.org):** The STEM Education Coalition supports teachers and students in STEM. The coalition works with educators to impart the critical role that STEM education plays in our country's economic prosperity and global competitiveness.

- **Technological Pedagogical and Content Knowledge (TPACK; www.tpck.org):** TPACK identifies and organizes knowledge educators need to effectively integrate technology to enhance pedagogy. Principals can use the TPACK image and conceptual model to better integrate technology into science instruction.

- **Topmarks Educational Search Engine:** These free interactive whiteboard resources are organized into age-appropriate categories (key stage 1: five- to seven-year-olds; key stage 2: seven- to eleven-year-olds).
    - Key stage 1 (www.topmarks.co.uk/Interactive.aspx?cat=62)
    - Key stage 2 (www.topmarks.co.uk/Interactive.aspx?cat=68)

Science Organizations

The following list provides a comprehensive summary of all major science organizations. Each site provides resources that can be used to enhance the science teaching.

- **American Association for the Advancement of Science (AAAS; www.aaas.org):** The AAAS publishes *Science* and is dedicated to advancing science around the world. The AAAS offers various resources for science education from news and current events to activities for teachers.

- **American Association of Physics Teachers (AAPT; www.aapt.org):** The AAPT centers research on enhancing the understanding of physical science. This site offers resources, news, and publications dealing with physics education.

- **American Chemical Society (ACS; www.acs.org):** The ACS offers information for all aspects of chemistry. Chemists and teachers alike will find a wealth of resources pertaining to all things chemistry.

- **American Geosciences Institute (AGI; www.agiweb.org):** The American Geosciences Institute offers curriculum guides, worksheets, and other useful information in geology-related sciences.

- **Department of Energy (DOE; www.energy.gov):** The DOE has an entire section dedicated to science education. There are also straightforward explanations to various types of energy, including renewable energy.

- **Environmental Protection Agency (EPA; www.epa.gov):** The Environmental Protection Agency provides leading-edge resources about science and technology, including information on air, climate change, ecosystems, health, and more.

- **Geological Society of America (GSA; www.geosociety.org):** This website provides a wealth of geology resources, including information on K–12 education as well as awards and grant opportunities.

- **International Council of Associations for Science Education (ICASE; www.icaseonline.net):** This organization was formed to improve science education worldwide. The site offers useful resources, such as presecondary science information, links to science lessons, and ICASE projects.

- **National Aeronautics and Space Administration (NASA; www.nasa.gov):** NASA is an important topic for all teachers focusing on astronomy. The website offers information on NASA missions and a huge collection of multimedia that will be sure to excite students of any age.

- **National Association of Biology Teachers (NABT; www.nabt.org):** This website provides tons of information for the life science teacher, including science resources and conference information.

- **National Association of Geoscience Teachers (NAGT; http://nagt.org):** This site offers information and activities geared to specific geographic regions. There is also a wide array of teacher resources available.

- **National Earth Science Teachers Association (NESTA; www.nestanet.org):** This nonprofit organization offers resources to further earth and space science education.

- **National Institute of Standards and Technology (NIST; www.nist.gov):** This informative site holds information from all science disciplines.

- **National Marine Educators Association (NMEA; www.marine-ed.org):** This site is dedicated to marine science education.

- **National Middle Level Science Teachers Association (NMLSTA; www.nmlsta.org):** The NMLSTA is specifically geared to middle school science teachers.

- **National Oceanic and Atmospheric Administration (NOAA; www.noaa.gov):** This site has tons of information pertaining to weather that can help bring relevance to lessons, including videos and live weather maps.

- **National Science Foundation (NSF; www.nsf.gov):** The NSF offers a wealth of science statistics that can be used for classroom activities.

- **Occupational Safety and Health Administration (OSHA; www.osha.gov):** This site has information on hazardous materials and the containment of these materials. It is a good website to help organize your chemical storage.

- **School Science and Mathematics Association (SSMA; www.ssma.org):** Information on the SSMA's publications, and their national convention.

- **U.S. Geological Survey (USGS; www.usgs.gov):** This site has grade-level information about science as well as lesson plans, teaching modules, and images with current data.

APPENDIX C
STATE PROFESSIONAL SCIENCE TEACHER ASSOCIATIONS

In addition to turning to the National Science Teachers Association for resources, teachers can use their state's professional science teacher association. Table C.1 lists each state's organization as well as its website.

Table C.1: State Professional Science Teacher Associations

State	Science Organization	Website
National	National Science Teachers Association	www.nsta.org
Alabama	Alabama Science Teachers Association	https://fp.auburn.edu/asta
Alaska	Alaska Science Teachers Association	www.aksta.org
Arizona	Arizona Science Teachers Association	www.azsta.org
Arkansas	Arkansas Science Teachers Association	www.arkscience.org
California	California Science Teachers Association	www.cascience.org/csta/csta.asp
Colorado	Colorado Association of Science Teachers	www.coloradocast.org
Connecticut	Connecticut Science Teachers Association	www.csta-us.org
Delaware	Delaware Teachers of Science	www.dts.k12.de.us
Florida	Florida Association of Science Teachers	www.fastscience.org
Georgia	Georgia Science Teachers Association	www.georgiascienceteacher.org
Hawaii	Hawaii Science Teachers Association	www.hasta.us
Idaho	Idaho Science Teachers Association	www.idscienceteachers.org
Illinois	Illinois Science Teachers Association	www.ista-il.org
Indiana	Hoosier Association of Science Teachers	www.hasti.org
Iowa	Iowa Academy of Science	www.iacad.org
Kansas	Kansas Association of Teachers of Science	http://kats.org

continued →

State	Science Organization	Website
Kentucky	Kentucky Science Teachers Association	www.ksta.org
Louisiana	Louisiana Science Teachers Association	www.lsta.info/index.php
Maine	Maine Science Teachers Association	https://sites.google.com/site/scienceteachersme
Maryland	Maryland Association of Science Teachers	www.emast.org
Massachusetts	Massachusetts Association of Science Teachers	www.massscienceteach.org
Michigan	Michigan Science Teachers Association	www.msta-mich.org
Minnesota	Minnesota Science Teachers Association	www.mnsta.org
Mississippi	Mississippi Science Teacher's Association	www.ms-scienceteachers.org
Missouri	Science Teachers of Missouri	www.stom.org
Montana	Montana Science Teachers Association	www.montanascience.org
Nebraska	Nebraska Association of Teachers of Science	http://nebraskaacademyofsciences.wildapricot.org/NATS
Nevada	Nevada State Science Teacher Association	www.nvscience.org
New Hampshire	New Hampshire Science Teachers' Association	www.nhsta.net
New Jersey	New Jersey Science Teachers Association	www.njsta.org
New Mexico	New Mexico Science Teachers Association	www.nmsta.org
New York	Science Teachers Association of New York State	www.stanys.org
North Carolina	North Carolina Science Teachers Association	www.ncsta.org
North Dakota	North Dakota Science Teachers Association	www.ndsta.k12.nd.us/index.htm
Ohio	Science Education Council of Ohio	www.secoonline.org
Oklahoma	Oklahoma Science Teachers Association	www.oklahomascienceteachersassociation.org
Oregon	Oregon Science Teachers Association	www.oregonscience.org
Pennsylvania	Pennsylvania Science Teachers Association	www.pascience.org
Rhode Island	RIScienceTeachers	http://riscienceteachers.wikispaces.com
South Carolina	South Carolina Science Council	www.southcarolinascience.org
South Dakota	South Dakota Science Teachers' Association	www.sdsta.org
Tennessee	Tennessee Science Teachers Association	www.tnsta.com
Texas	Science Teachers Association of Texas	www.statweb.org
Utah	Utah Science Teachers Association	www.utahscienceteachers.org/Home.html
Vermont	Vermont Science Teachers Association	www.uvm.edu/vsta
Virginia	Virginia Association of Science Teachers	www.vast.org
Washington	Washington Science Teachers Association	www.wsta.net
West Virginia	West Virginia Science Teachers Association	www.wvsta.org
Wisconsin	Wisconsin Society of Science Teachers	www.wsst.org
Wyoming	Wyoming Science Teachers Association	http://w3.tribcsp.com/~wsta

Source: NSTA, 2011b.

APPENDIX D
SCIENCE CONTENT STANDARDS FOR INQUIRY

According to the NRC (1996), scientific inquiry is

> the diverse ways in which scientists study the natural world and propose explanations based on the evidence derived from their work. It also refers to the activities through which students develop knowledge and understanding of scientific ideas, as well as an understanding of how scientists study the natural world. (p. 23)

The following science content standards establish a foundation for promoting inquiry during the teaching and learning process.

Fundamental Abilities Necessary to Do Scientific Inquiry

The following section lists specific strategies and ideas to establish a teaching and learning culture that promotes and supports inquiry-based science. Scientific inquiry should increase in complexity as students progress from grade levels.

Grades K–4
- Ask a question about objects, organisms, and events in the environment.
- Plan and conduct a simple investigation.
- Employ simple equipment and tools to gather data and extend the senses.
- Use data to construct a reasonable explanation.
- Communicate investigations and explanations.

Grades 5–8
- Identify questions that can be answered through scientific investigations.

- Design and conduct a scientific investigation.
- Use appropriate tools and techniques to gather, analyze, and interpret data.
- Develop descriptions, explanations, predictions, and models using evidence.
- Think critically and logically to make the relationships between evidence and explanations.
- Recognize and analyze alternative explanations and predictions.
- Communicate scientific procedures and explanations.
- Use mathematics in all aspects of scientific inquiry.

Fundamental Understandings About Scientific Inquiry

In order to properly implement inquiry-based learning in science, principals and teachers need to have an understanding of the fundamental aspects of scientific inquiry. The following list provides guidelines for principals to assist teachers in constructing pedagogically sound learning activities that incorporate scientific inquiry.

Grades K–4

- Scientific investigations involve asking and answering a question and comparing the answer with what scientists already know about the world.
- Scientists use different kinds of investigations depending on the questions they are trying to answer. Types of investigations include describing objects, events, and organisms; classifying them; and doing a fair test (experimenting).
- Simple instruments, such as magnifiers, thermometers, and rulers, provide more information than scientists obtain using only their senses.
- Scientists make the results of their investigations public; they describe the investigations in ways that enable others to repeat the investigations.
- Scientists develop explanations using observations (evidence) and what they already know about the world (scientific knowledge). Good explanations are based on evidence from investigations.
- Scientists review and ask questions about the results of other scientists' work.

Grades 5–8

- Different kinds of questions suggest different kinds of scientific investigations. Some investigations involve observing and describing objects, organisms, or events; some involve collecting specimens; some involve experiments; some involve seeking more information; some involve discovery of new objects and phenomena; and some involve making models.

- Current scientific knowledge and understanding guide scientific investigations. Different scientific domains employ different methods, core theories, and standards to advance scientific knowledge and understanding.

- Mathematics is important in all aspects of scientific inquiry.

- Technology used to gather data enhances accuracy and allows scientists to analyze and quantify results of investigations.

- Scientific explanations emphasize evidence, have logically consistent arguments, and use scientific principles, models, and theories. The scientific community accepts and uses such explanations until better scientific theories replace them. When such displacement occurs, science advances.

- Science advances through legitimate skepticism. Asking questions and querying other scientists' explanations are part of scientific inquiry. Scientists evaluate other scientists' explanations by examining evidence, comparing evidence, identifying faulty reasoning, pointing out statements that go beyond the evidence, and suggesting alternative explanations for the same observations.

- Scientific investigations sometimes result in new ideas and phenomena for study, generate new methods or procedures for an investigation, or develop new technologies to improve the collection of data. All of these results can lead to new investigations.

Source: Adapted from NRC, 1996, 2000.

APPENDIX E
SAMPLE K-2 SCIENCE ACTIVITY: THE MYSTERY BOX

Source: Michaels, Shouse, & Schweingruber, 2008, pp. 66–69. Adapted with permission from National Academies Press, Copyright 2008, National Academy of Sciences.

"Are you ready to run a Mystery Box investigation with me?" Ms. Winter asked as her twenty-two kindergartners gathered around her. The classroom erupted into cheers. "Look at all these different balloons that I brought in." She pointed to two identical sets of balloons—each of a different color, and each with a different substance inside. There were three red balloons, and three green balloons. Inside one green and one red was water, another green and another red was ice, and inside another green and another red was just air. Each set was lined up in a row in front of a wooden chest a little bigger than a toaster. The box was latched shut with a heavy lock, and a key tied to a long ribbon was next to the box (see figure E.1).

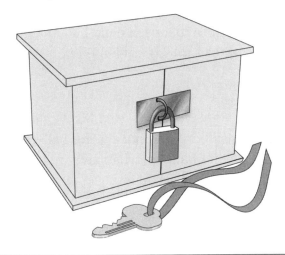

Figure E.1: The Mystery Box.

"One set of these balloons is going to be mine, and the other set is going to be yours," Ms. Winter said. She quickly established with the children balloons. "So," she summed up, "we have a green and a red balloon with water, a green and a red balloon filled with ice, and a green and a red balloon with air."

"Now, I'm going to take my whole set away," she said, scooping up all of her balloons and tossing them into a bag. "Then, I'm going to take one item—just one—from my set and put it into the Mystery Box. Close your eyes. No peeking!" All twenty-two kindergartners gleefully covered their eyes.

Ms. Winter turned her back to the kids, unlocked the Mystery Box, selected a balloon from her bag, and locked it inside the box with the key. The students' set of six items—red and green balloons—remained lined up in front of the Mystery Box.

"Now open your eyes," she said. "Inside the Mystery Box is one thing taken from my set of objects, which is just like your set. And here's the amazing thing. You're going to figure out what is inside the Mystery Box just by asking me questions." Then, very dramatically, Ms. Winter uttered the words she always used to start the Mystery Box game. "If you ask me a question about what's inside the Mystery Box, I will tell you the truth."

"I know," said Maya. "Is it a red balloon with air?"

"That is a very good question, Maya. Do you know why it's a good question? It's a good question because . . . it's *not* the red balloon with air." Several kids giggled; a few sighed with disappointment.

"So Maya's question has taught us something important," Ms. Winter said. "Whatever is inside the box, it is not the red balloon with air. So, that means we don't need this one here anymore." She picked up the red balloon with air from the students' set of balloons and put it on the table out of sight.

Ms. Winter reached into a cup of Popsicle sticks that had all of the children's names written on them, which she used to ensure that each child had an equal chance of getting a turn. The stick she pulled from the cup had *Carlos* written on it.

"Is it a water balloon?" Carlos asked.

"Is it a water balloon? Carlos wants to know," said Ms. Winter. "That's another good question, because what is in the Mystery Box . . . is *not* a water balloon." The children laughed and clapped. "And because it's not a water balloon, what have we learned?" Ms. Winter picked up the red water balloon and the green water balloon.

"We don't need them," two children said.

"Right. Because we know it's not a water balloon in our box, we can get rid of every water balloon. It can't be one of these." Ms. Winter put the two water balloons out of sight.

Sample K–2 Science Activity: The Mystery Box

"Hey, I just noticed something interesting," said Ms. Winter. "With Maya's question we got rid of one thing, the red air balloon. With Carlos's question, we got rid of *two* things, both water balloons. Can anyone figure out why that is?" No one said anything. Ms. Winter waited.

Finally, Kelly, who tended not to talk much in the large group, raised her hand. "Carlos asked about all of the balloons, and Maya just asked about the red one with air."

"Wow! Did anyone hear what Kelly said?"

Lots of hands went up.

"Does anyone think they can put what Kelly said in their own words? Yes, James?"

"She said Carlos asked his question about *all* the water balloons. Maya asked about only one balloon—the red air balloon. It's like we got three answers with one question."

"Is that what you were saying, Kelly?"

Kelly nodded.

"Wow, you guys are really thinking today. I can see smoke coming out of your ears. Let's see who's next?"

Ms. Winter selected another Popsicle stick that said *Hayley* on it. "Hayley, what would you like to ask?"

"Is it an ice balloon?" Hayley asked.

"That's a very good question. Do you know why? Because, I'm telling you the truth, it is *not* an ice balloon!"

The kids squealed with delight. Ms. Winter removed the two ice balloons from the students' set, leaving only one balloon. She then selected one more Popsicle stick.

"Decklan, what question would you like to ask?"

Decklan pronounced, "I don't need to ask a question because the only balloon left is the green balloon with air in it!"

"Are you sure, Decklan?" Ms. Winter asked.

"A billion percent," called out Decklan. Slowly and dramatically, Ms. Winter removed the lock and opened the doors of the Mystery Box, revealing—"Ta-da!"—the green air balloon inside.

"Congratulations," Ms. Winter said. "Just by asking questions, without being able to see inside, you've discovered what's in the Mystery Box." Ms. Winter's twenty-two kindergartners broke into applause.

GLOSSARY

assessment. Determining what is known and not known. Assessment does not judge the value of what was analyzed.

benchmarks. Benchmarks, sometimes called *objectives*, are more specific than standards or goals. They are milestones or checkpoints on a student's journey to achieve the standard or goal.

Bloom's Taxonomy. A six-level cognitive hierarchy that categorizes learning and thinking from lower-level to higher-level knowledge, comprehension, application, analysis, synthesis, and evaluation.

confirmatory assessment. Assessment an outside agency does at a later time to determine how enduring learning is.

constant. Variables that are held constant and therefore not allowed to change during the experiment.

constructivist learning cycle. A science teaching strategy that engages students in inquiry-based learning through a cyclical process that has them explore, construct explanations, and apply what they have learned to new situations.

control. The comparison group. Though the control group can be any group, the term is usually assigned to the group that receives no treatment.

dependent variable. A variable that responds to the manipulated variable.

diagnostic assessment. Assessing student learning at the beginning of instruction in order to determine what students know or are able to do. The information gained is used to guide instruction.

discrepant events. Demonstrations used to introduce science phenomena that are contrary to what would be commonly expected.

essential questions. Questions that are not answerable with finality in a brief sentence whose aim is to stimulate thought, provoke inquiry, and spark more questions.

evaluation. Assessment for the purpose of evaluating the quality of performance. It sets a value on the performance.

experimental design. A process for designing and organizing scientifically accurate laboratory experiments.

formative assessment. Assessment of student learning during the process of learning in order to guide instruction.

goals. Goals, sometimes called *standards*, are broad statements of what students should know and be able to do after completing a set course of study.

hands-on. Students manipulating real science materials, when safe and appropriate, in ways similar to scientists.

hypothesis. An educated guess for the outcome of an experiment. It is often written as an "if, then" statement.

independent variable. A variable that the experimenter purposefully manipulates or changes. It is often referred to as the "I" variable because it starts with *i* and is the variable that "I" set, and the one "I" determine the quantities for.

indicators. Indicators are observable behaviors that are specific to a benchmark or objective. Indicators are specific classroom behaviors that provide evidence that a student understands or can apply science content to solve problems or build a larger knowledge base.

inquiry. The process of asking questions, exploring natural phenomena, conducting experiments, finding patterns in data, seeking information, and solving problems.

kit-based. A complete set of hands-on science experiments and printed materials packaged for a coherent unit of instruction.

knowledge. Facts, concepts, theories, laws, and models.

nature of science. Attitudes and beliefs scientists share about science and scientific investigation, such as the belief that through careful observation and systematic study scientific ideas and theories change over time as new knowledge is discovered and new patterns are identified.

objectives. Objectives, sometimes called *benchmarks*, are more specific than standards or goals. They are milestones or checkpoints on a student's journey to achieve the standard or goal.

prediction. A guess for the outcome of a demonstration or event.

process skills. In the process of seeking evidence to support conclusions, scientists tend to use similar process skills, such as observing, measuring, estimating, classifying, comparing, organizing, predicting, analyzing, inferring, forming hypotheses, and experimenting.

repeated trials. Conducting the experiment multiple times to ensure accuracy.

standards. Standards, sometimes called *goals*, are broad statements of what students should know and be able to do after completing a set course of study.

STEM. Science, technology, engineering, and mathematics.

summative assessment. Is usually evaluative and done at the end of a course of study for a grade.

understanding. The integration of knowledge into useful relationships and applications that explain and predict.

wait time. The time between when a teacher asks a question and a student responds, or the time between when a student responds and the teacher comments further.

REFERENCES AND RESOURCES

American Association for the Advancement of Science. (1989). *Science for all Americans: A Project 2061 report on literacy goals in science, mathematics, and technology.* Washington, DC: Author.

American Association for the Advancement of Science. (1993). *Benchmarks for science literacy.* New York: Oxford University Press. Accessed at www.project2061.org/publications/bsl/online/index.php on February 10, 2012.

American Association for the Advancement of Science. (1997). *Resources for science literacy: Professional development.* New York: Oxford University Press.

American Chemical Society. (2003). *Safety in academic chemistry laboratories.* Washington, DC: Author.

Anderson, W. A., Banerjee, U., Drennan, C. L., Elgin, S. C. R., Epstein, I. R., Handelsman, J., et al. (2011). Changing the culture of science education at research universities. *Science, 331*(6014), 152–153.

Annenberg Foundation. (1997). *Case studies in science education* [Video series]. Accessed at www.learner.org/resources/series21.html on June 28, 2011.

Armstrong, T. (1994). *Multiple intelligences in the classroom.* Alexandria, VA: Association for Supervision and Curriculum Development.

Baker, L. (2004). Reading comprehension and science inquiry: Metacognitive connections. In E. W. Saul (Ed.), *Crossing borders in literacy and science instruction: Perspectives on theory and practice* (pp. 239–257). Newark, DE: International Reading Association.

Barnett, M., Yamagata-Lynch, L., Keating, T., Barab, S. A., & Hay, K. E. (2005). Using virtual reality computer models to support student understanding of astronomical concepts. *Journal of Computers in Mathematics and Science Teaching, 24*(4), 333–356.

Baxter Magolda, M. B. (1999). *Creating contexts for learning and self-authorship: Constructive-developmental pedagogy.* Nashville, TN: Vanderbilt University Press.

Bayer Corporation. (2010). *A compendium of best practice K–12 STEM education programs.* Accessed at www.mos.org/nctl/news_article.php?r=5166 on May 12, 2012.

Blackmore, P., & Cousin, G. (2003). Linking teaching and research through research-based learning. *Educational Developments, 4*(4), 24–27.

Bransford, J. D., Brown, A. L., & Cocking, R. R. (Eds.). (1999). *How people learn: Brain, mind, experience, and school.* Washington, DC: National Academies Press.

Burgstahler, S. (2009). *Making science labs accessible to students with disabilities.* Seattle: University of Washington.

Cakir, M. (2008). Constructivist approaches to learning science and their implications for science pedagogy: A literature review. *International Journal of Environmental and Science Education, 3*(4), 193–206.

Calhoun, E. F. (1994). *How to use action research in the self-renewing school.* Alexandria, VA: Association for Supervision and Curriculum Development.

Checkovich, B. H., & Sterling, D. R. (2001). Oh say can you see. *Science and Children, 38*(4), 32–35.

Cothron, J. H., Giese, R. N., & Rezba, R. J. (2000). *Students and research: Practical strategies for science classrooms and competitions.* Dubuque, IA: Kendall/Hunt.

Donovan, M. S., & Bransford, J. D. (Eds.). (2005). *How students learn: History, mathematics, and science in the classroom.* Washington, DC: National Academies Press.

Educational Research Service. (1999). *Improving student achievement in science.* Arlington, VA: Author.

English, F. W. (1988). *Curriculum auditing.* Lancaster, PA: Technomic.

Farenga, S. J., Joyce, B. A., & Dowling, T. W. (2002). Rocketing into adaptive inquiry. *Science Scope, 25*(4), 34–39.

Flinn Scientific. (2002). *Chemical and biological catalog reference manual.* Batavia, IL: Author.

Flinn Scientific. (2012). General laboratory safety. Accessed at www.flinnsci.com/sections/safety/safety.asp on July 18, 2012.

Foley, B. J., & McPhee, C. (2008). *Students' attitudes towards science in classes using hands-on or textbook based curriculum.* Accessed at www.csun.edu/~bfoley/Foley&McPhee%20AERA08.pdf on February 9, 2012.

Gall, M. D., & Vojtek, R. O. (1994). *Planning for effective staff development: Six research-based models.* Eugene, OR: ERIC Clearinghouse on Educational Management.

Gardner, H. (1983). *Frames of mind: The theory of multiple intelligences.* New York: Basic Books.

Hestenes, D. (1996, August). *Modeling methodology for physics teachers.* Paper presented at the International Conference on Undergraduate Physics Education, College Park, MD.

Holistic Education Network of Tasmania. (n.d.). *Scientific inquiry process.* Accessed at www.hent.org/sue/Scientific%20Inquiry%20Process.htm on February 10, 2012.

Hord, S. M. (2009). Professional learning communities. *National Staff Development Council, 30*(1), 40–42. Accessed at http://sectorleaderswaikato.wikispaces.com/file/view/Professional+Learning+Communities+Hord.pdf on July 20, 2011.

Jacobs, H. H. (2010). *Curriculum 21: Essential education for a changing world.* Alexandria, VA: Association for Supervision and Curriculum Development.

Krajcik, J. S., & Sutherland, L. M. (2010). Supporting students in developing literacy in science. *Science, 328*(5977), 456–459.

Lederman, N. G. (1999). Teachers' understanding of the nature of science and classroom practice: Factors that facilitate or impede the relationship. *Journal of Research in Science Teaching, 36*(8), 916–929.

Lederman, N. G., & Lederman, S. J. (2004). Revising instruction to teach nature of science. *The Science Teacher, 71*(9), 36–39.

Leithwood, K., Louis, K. S., Anderson, S., & Wahlstrom, K. (2004). *How leadership influences student learning.* Minneapolis, MN: Center for Applied Research and Educational Improvement.

Levy, F., & Murnane, R. J. (2004). *The new division of labor: How computers are creating the next job market.* Princeton, NJ: Princeton University Press.

Loucks-Horsley, S., Hewson, P. W., Love, N., & Stiles, K. E. (1998). *Designing professional development for teachers of science and mathematics.* Thousand Oaks, CA: Corwin Press.

Marczely, B. (1996). *Personalizing professional growth: Staff development that works.* Thousand Oaks, CA: Corwin Press.

Metz, S. (2011). Promoting STEM careers starts in the K–12 classroom. *ASCD Express, 6*(24). Accessed at www.ascd.org/ascd-express/vol6/624-metz.aspx on February 9, 2012.

Michaels, S., Shouse, A. W., & Schweingruber, H. A. (2008). *Ready, set, science! Putting research to work in K–8 science classrooms.* Washington, DC: National Academies Press.

Moore, B., & Stanley, T. (2010). *Critical thinking and formative assessments: Increasing rigor in your classroom.* Larchmont, NY: Eye on Education.

Mullis, I. V. S., Martin, M. O., Smith, T. A., Ruddock, G. J., O'Sullivan, C. Y., & Preuschoff, C. (2011). *TIMSS 2011 assessment frameworks.* Chestnut Hill, MA: Boston College.

National Center for Education Statistics. (1999). *Trends in international mathematics and science study.* Accessed at http://nces.ed.gov/timss/video.asp on July 23, 2011.

National Council of Teachers of Mathematics. (2011). *The metric system: A position of NCTM.* Accessed at www.nctm.org/uploadedFiles/About_NCTM/Position_Statements/Metric_System_Positions_Statement_20113.pdf#search=%22metrication position%22 on July 23, 2011.

National Governors Association Center for Best Practices & Council of Chief State School Officers. (2012). *Mission statement.* Accessed at www.corestandards.org on June 30, 2012.

National Research Council. (1996). *National Science Education Standards: Observe, interact, change, learn.* Washington, DC: National Academies Press. Accessed at www.nap.edu/openbook.php?record_id=4962 on April 4, 2012.

National Research Council. (1999). *Designing mathematics or science curriculum programs: A guide for using mathematics and science education standards.* Washington, DC: National Academies Press.

National Research Council. (2000). *Inquiry and the National Science Education Standards: A guide for teaching and learning.* Washington, DC: National Academies Press.

National Research Council. (2006). *America's lab report: Investigations in high school science.* Washington, DC: National Academies Press.

National Research Council. (2007). *Taking science to school: Learning and teaching science in grades K–8.* Washington, DC: National Academies Press.

National Research Council. (2012). *A framework for K–12 science education: Practices, crosscutting concepts, and core ideas.* Washington, DC: National Academies Press. Accessed at www.nap.edu/openbook.php?record_id=13165&page=1 on April 4, 2012.

National Science Teachers Association. (1998). *NSTA position statement: The national science education standards.* Accessed at www.nsta.org/about/positions/standards.aspx on February 9, 2012.

National Science Teachers Association. (1999). *NSTA position statement: Use of the metric system.* Accessed at www.nsta.org/about/positions/metric.aspx on February 9, 2012.

National Science Teachers Association. (2000a). *NSTA position statement: The nature of science.* Accessed at www.nsta.org/about/positions/natureofscience.aspx on February 9, 2012.

National Science Teachers Association. (2000b). *NSTA position statement: Safety and school science instruction.* Accessed at www.nsta.org/about/positions/safety.aspx on February 9, 2012.

National Science Teachers Association. (2002). *About NSTA: The executive summary.* Accessed at www.nsta.org/about on February 9, 2012.

National Science Teachers Association. (2003). *NSTA position statement: Gender equity in science education.* Accessed at www.nsta.org/about/positions/genderequity.aspx on May 12, 2012.

National Science Teachers Association. (2007a). *NSTA position statement: The integral role of laboratory investigations in science instruction.* Accessed at www.nsta.org/about/positions/laboratory.aspx on February 9, 2012.

National Science Teachers Association. (2007b). *NSTA position statement: Liability of science educators for laboratory safety.* Accessed at www.nsta.org/about/positions/liability.aspx on March 5, 2012.

National Science Teachers Association. (2010). *NSTA position statement: The role of research on science teaching and learning.* Accessed at www.nsta.org/about/positions/research.aspx on February 9, 2012.

National Science Teachers Association. (2011a). *NSTA position statement: Quality science education and 21st-century skills.* Accessed at www.nsta.org/about/positions/21stcentury.aspx on February 9, 2012.

National Science Teachers Association. (2011b). *Professional collaboration: Chapters and associated groups.* Accessed at www.nsta.org/about/collaboration/chapters on July 25, 2011.

National Science Teachers Association. (2012). *Outstanding science trade books for students K–12.* Accessed at www.nsta.org/publications/ostb on February 10, 2012.

Newmann, F. M., Smith, B., Allensworth, E., & Bryk, A. S. (2001). *School instructional program coherence: Benefits and challenges.* Chicago: Consortium on Chicago School Research. Accessed at http://ccsr.uchicago.edu/publications/p0d02.pdf on February 9, 2012.

Norris, S. P., & Phillips, L. M. (2003). How literacy in its fundamental sense is central to scientific literacy. *Science Education, 87*(2), 224–240.

Occupational Safety and Health Administration, 29 C.F.R. § 1910.1450d (1974).

Occupational Safety and Health Administration, 29 C.F.R. § 1910.1200 (1987).

Ogan-Bekiroglu, F. (2007). Bridging the gap: Needs assessment of science teacher in-service education in Turkey and the effects of teacher and school demographics. *Journal of Education for Teaching: International Research and Pedagogy, 33*(4), 44–456.

Pegg, J. (2010). Integrating literacy into elementary science: Teacher concerns and their resolutions. *The Electronic Journal of Literacy Through Science, 9*(1), 1–14.

Priest, R. H., & Sterling, D. R. (2001). Integrating technology. *The Science Teacher, 68*(3), 61–64.

Rowe, M. B. (1974). Wait-time and rewards as instructional variables: Their influence on language, logic, and fate control. *Journal of Research in Science Teaching, 11*(2), 81–94.

Shulman, L. S. (1987). Knowledge and teaching: Foundations of the new reform. *Harvard Educational Review, 57*(1), 1–22.

Squires, D. A. (2009). *Curriculum alignment: Research-based strategies for increasing student achievement.* Thousand Oaks, CA: Corwin Press.

Sterling, D. R. (1996). Science in the news. *Science Scope, 19*(5), 22–24.

Sterling, D. R. (1998). Getting students to measure up. *Science Scope, 21*(5), 14–17.

Sterling, D. R. (1999a). Measuring skills. *The Science Teacher, 66*(1), 58–62.

Sterling, D. R. (1999b). Third International Mathematics and Science Study (TIMSS) and the nature of college courses. *The Journal of Mathematics and Science, 2*(2), 39–45.

Sterling, D. R. (2002, April). *Strategies enabling teachers to assess student understanding of science.* Paper presented at the annual conference of the American Educational Research Association, New Orleans, LA.

Stevens, F., Lawrenz, F., & Sharp, L. (1993). *User-friendly handbook for project evaluation: Science, mathematics, engineering, and technology education.* Arlington, VA: National Science Foundation.

Stewart, V. (2010). A classroom as wide as the world. In H. H. Jacobs (Ed.), *Curriculum 21: Essential education for a changing world* (pp. 97–114). Alexandria, VA: Association for Supervision and Curriculum Development.

Sweeney, J. (1988). *Tips for improving school climate.* Arlington, VA: American Association of School Administrators.

Trowbridge, L. W., Bybee, R. W., & Powell, J. C. (2000). *Teaching secondary school science: Strategies for developing scientific literacy* (7th ed.). Upper Saddle River, NJ: Merrill.

U.S. Department of Education. (1999a). *Designing effective professional development: Lessons from the Eisenhower program.* Washington, DC: U.S. Government Printing Office.

U.S. Department of Education. (1999b). *The TIMSS videotape classroom study: Methods and findings from an exploratory research project on eighth-grade mathematics instruction in Germany, Japan, and the United States* (NCES 99–074). Washington, DC: U.S. Government Printing Office.

U.S. Department of Education. (2000). *Before it's too late: A report to the nation from the National Commission on Mathematics and Science Teaching for the 21st Century.* Jessup, MD: Education Publications Center. Accessed at www2.ed.gov/inits/Math/glenn/report.pdf on February 9, 2012.

U.S. Department of Education. (2008). *Trends in international mathematics and science study (TIMSS).* Accessed at http://nces.ed.gov/timss/index.asp on February 9, 2012.

U.S. Department of Education. (2011). *The nation's report card: The national assessment of educational progress.* Accessed at http://nces.ed.gov/nationsreportcard on August 5, 2011.

U.S. Department of Labor Occupational Safety and Health Administration. (1996). *OSHA hazard communication standards.* Accessed at www.osha.gov/pls/oshaweb/owadisp.show_document?p_table=standards&p_id=10099 on March 21, 2012.

Venkataraman, B., Riordan, D. G., & Olson, S. (2010). *Prepare and inspire: K–12 education in science, technology, engineering, and math (STEM) for America's future.* Washington, DC: President's Council of Advisors on Science and Technology.

West, S. S., Westerlund, J. F., Stephenson, A. L., & Nelson, N. (2005). Conditions that affect secondary science safety: Results from 2001 Texas survey, overcrowding. *The Texas Science Teacher, 34*(1), 21–31.

Wetzel, D. R., & Sterling, D. R. (1998). Laser labs. *Science Scope, 22*(3), 34–35.

The White House, Office of the Press Secretary. (2009). *President Obama launches the "Educate to Innovate" campaign for excellence in science, technology, engineering, & math (stem) education* [Press release]. Accessed at www.whitehouse.gov/the-press-office/president-obama-launches-educate-innovate-campaign-excellence-science-technology-en on February 9, 2012.

Wiggins, G. P. (1993). *Assessing student performance.* San Francisco: Jossey-Bass.

Wiggins, G., & McTighe, J. (1998). *Understanding by design.* Alexandria, VA: Association for Supervision and Curriculum Development.

Wilmarth, S. (2010). Five socio-technology trends that change everything in learning and teaching. In H. H. Jacobs (Ed.), *Curriculum 21: Essential education for a changing world* (pp. 80–96). Alexandria, VA: Association for Supervision and Curriculum Development.

Wilson, E. A. (1995). *Reading at the middle and high school levels: Building active readers across the curriculum.* Arlington, VA: Educational Research Service.

Zucker, A. A., Tinker, R., Staudt, C., Mansfield, A., & Metcalf, S. (2008). Learning science in grades 3–8 using probeware and computers: Findings from the TEEMSS II Project. *Journal of Science Education and Technology, 17*(1), 42–48.

INDEX

A

Activities Integrating Mathematics and Science (AIMS), 24, 95
Allensworth, E., 18–20
All Things PLC, 69
American Association for the Advancement of Science (AAAS), 11, 47
American Chemical Society (ACS), 27, 28
American National Standards Institute (ANSI), 27
Anderson, S., 23
assessments
    authentic, 58–63
    checklist, 57, 63, 90–91, 94
    confirmatory, 58
    data collection, 56
    data use, 55–56
    data users, 56
    diagnostic, 57
    formative, 57–58
    role of, 55
    rubrics, 60–62, 63, 64
    summative, 58
    survey, 63, 82–83, 92
    techniques, 63–65
    timeline, 57
    See also self-assessment
authentic assessment, 58–63

B

Benchmarks for Science Literacy (AAAS), 11
best fit theory, 5
blogging, 51
Bloom's Taxonomy, 45
Bryk, A. S., 18–20
Burgstahler, S., 28

C

change, preparing for, 1–2
Children's Book Council, 24
CK–12 Foundation, 23
classroom environment, observation guidelines for, 88
climate, 1
    observation guidelines for classroom learning, 85, 89
    cognitive domains, 20–21
collaboration, teacher, 67–68
Common Core State Standards, 13–14
concept maps, 49
conceptual understanding, 21
confirmatory assessment, 58
Copernicus, 5
Cothron, J. H., 26
critical thinking, promoting, 45
curriculum
    adoption committee, 21
    alignment, 18–20
    cognitive domains, 20–21
    components of a coherent, 19
    content, familiarizing yourself with, 16–17
    content, when to teach, 17
    ensuring instruction follows program, 17–18
    materials and activities, selecting and evaluating, 21–29, 74–75
    role of principals, 16–18
    staff support, 18
    standards and categories, 15–16
    time scheduled for teaching, 17–18, 36–37
    variations in, 16

D

data collection, 56

data use, 55–56
data users, 56
diagnostic assessment, 57
Dowling, T. W., 42
Dropbox, 52

E

Educate to Innovate, 37
Educational Development Center, 24
educational resources, 98–100
Education Week, 71
Educator's PLN, 52
evaluation, program. *See* self-assessment
experimental design diagram, 26, 76

F

factual knowledge, 20
Farenga, S. J., 42
FAST (Foundational Approaches in Science Teaching), 23, 96
FlexBooks, 23
Flinn Scientific, 28
Foley, B. J., 23
formative assessment, 57–58
FOSS (Full Option Science System), 23–24, 95, 96
Foundational Approaches in Science Teaching (FAST), 23, 96
Full Option Science System (FOSS), 23–24, 95, 96

G

GEMS (Great Explorations in Math and Science), 24, 96
Giese, R. N., 26
global interaction, encouraging, 51–52
Google Docs, 50, 52
Google Talk, 52
Great Explorations in Math and Science (GEMS), 24, 96

H

hands-on learning, effective, 42–44

I

iChat, 52
inquiry-based teaching
    essential features of, 44
    hands-on learning, effective, 42–44
    promoting, 42–51
    strategies for improving student achievement, 44–51
Insights, 24, 96
instruction
    best practices, 48
    collaborative methods to improve, 41–42
    discussion guidelines and questions, 39, 79, 82–87
    indicators of ineffective, 84
    observation form, 40, 86–87, 90
    planning template, 80–81
    signs of ineffective, 40–41, 88
    strategies for improving, 44–51
    supporting teachers, 40
Internet, use of, 51–52

J

Joyce, B. A., 42

L

laboratory activities
    class-size recommendations, 27
    creating, 24–26
    in elementary and middle school, 45–47
    experimental design diagram, 26, 76
    goggles, use of safety, 27
    safety issues, 26–29
    students with disabilities and, 28
Lawrence Hall of Science, 23, 24
Learner, A., 70
Lederman, N., 5

M

materials and activities
    evaluation form, 74–75
    Mystery Box activity, 109–111
    selecting, 21–29
McPhee, C., 23

models, use of, 47–48
Mullis, I. V. S., 20–21
Mystery Box activity, 109–111

N

National Research Council (NRC), 7, 9, 10–11, 12, 15–16, 105
National Science Education Standards (NRC), 11, 14, 15, 24, 42, 67–68
National Science Resources Center, 24
National Science Teachers Association (NSTA), 5, 13, 24, 27
    hands-on learning and, 43
    lab activities in elementary and middle school and, 45–47
    publications and role of, 14
    quality education and skills statement, 49–50
    safety issues and, 29
Newmann, F. M., 18–20
Next Generation Science Standards, 14

O

Obama, B., 37
observation
    guidelines for classroom environment, 88
    guidelines for classroom learning climate, 85, 89
    of instruction, 40, 86–87, 90
    inventory survey, 63, 82–83
Olson, S., 37
OpenTexts, 23
organizations, 100–102
OSHA (Occupational Safety and Health Administration) Hazard Communication Standard, 27–28

P

patterns in data, identifying, 26
PhET, 51
probeware, 50, 97
professional teacher associations, 103–104
professional development
    barriers, 71
    goals of, 67–68
    principles of, 68
    process, 69–70
    programs, evaluating, 70–71, 93–94
    programs, planning, 68–69
    support for, 18
Promethean whiteboard, 51

Q

questioning techniques, critical thinking and, 45

R

reading, integrating into content-area instruction, 49
reasoning and analysis, 21
relational study, 23
research-supported practices, 52–53
Rezba, R. J., 26
Riordan, D. G., 37
rubrics, 60–62, 63, 64

S

safety issues, lab, 26–29
science, nature of, 8–9
Science and Technology Concepts for Middle Schools (STC/MS), 24, 96
Science and Technology Concepts (STC), 24, 96
science education, renewed interest in, 3
science events, self-assessment and use of, 36
Science for All Americans (AAAS), 11
Science Fusion, 97
science kits, 23–24
Science Matters, 14
Science News, 51
Science News for Kids, 51
Science Notebooks in K–12 Classrooms, 49
science reform movement, origins of, 11
scientific inquiry (investigation)
    abilities necessary to do, 105–106
    basics of, 106–107
    defined, 6–7, 105
    example of, 7–8
    global consensus, 9–14

principles and goals for K–8 programs, 9–11
scientific knowledge, defined, 5
scientific literacy, 7, 49
scientific method, 6
self-assessment
    data to use in, 36–37
    scenario examples, 33–36
    survey, 31–33, 63, 77–78
    See also assessments
simulations, 51, 97
Skype, 52
SMART whiteboard, 51
Smith, B., 18–20
Sputnik, 3
standardized test scores, self-assessment and use of, 36
standards
    Common Core State, 13–14
    content, 107
    development of national, 11–12
    science education, 11
STC (Science and Technology Concepts), 24, 96
STC/MS (Science and Technology Concepts for Middle Schools), 24, 96
STEM (science, technology, engineering, and mathematics), 3, 12–13, 37
Sterling, D. R., 58
student grades, self-assessment and use of, 36
Students and Research (Cothron, Giese, and Rezba), 26
students with disabilities, lab activities and, 28
summative assessment, 58

T

Teacher Learner Community, 71
teachers
    collaboration, 67–68
    supporting, 40
    See also professional development
teamwork. See professional development
technology
    resources, 97
    use of, 50–52, 97
textbooks, effective use of, 22–23
trade books, 24
Trends in International Mathematics and Science Study (TIMSS), 9, 70
Twitter, 51–52

U

U.S. Department of Education, 22, 23

V

Venkataraman, B., 37
video conferencing, 52

W

whiteboards, 51, 98
writing, integrating into content-area instruction, 49

What Principals Need to Know About the Basics of Creating Brain-Compatible Classrooms
David A. Sousa
Understand the basics for creating a brain-compatible classroom with this brief, accessible guide customized for principals. This book provides an overview of educational neuroscience designed to help principals construct meaningful professional development that enhances teachers' knowledge and skills about brain-compatible learning.
BKF463

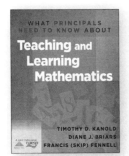

What Principals Need to Know About Teaching and Learning Mathematics
Timothy D. Kanold, Diane J. Briars, and Francis (Skip) Fennell
This must-have resource offers support and encouragement for improved mathematics achievement across every grade level. With an emphasis on Principles and Standards for School Mathematics and Common Core State Standards, this book covers the importance of mathematics content, learning and instruction, and mathematics assessment.
BKF501

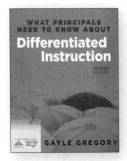

What Principals Need to Know About Differentiated Instruction, 2nd Edition
Gayle Gregory
This valuable resource gives administrators the knowledge and skills needed to enable teachers to implement and sustain differentiation. Learn information and strategies to jump-start, guide, and coach teachers as they respond to the needs of diverse students.
BKF536

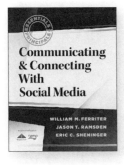

Communicating & Connecting With Social Media
William M. Ferriter, Jason T. Ramsden, and Eric C. Sheninger
In this short text, the authors examine how enterprising schools are using social media tools to provide customized professional development for teachers and to transform communication practices with staff, students, parents, and other stakeholders.
BKF474

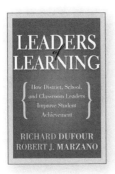

Leaders of Learning
Richard DuFour and Robert J. Marzano
Together, the authors focus on district leadership, principal leadership, and team leadership and address how individual teachers can be most effective in leading students—by learning with colleagues how to implement the most promising pedagogy in their classrooms.
BKF455

Solution Tree | Press Visit solution-tree.com or call 800.733.6786 to order.

Solution Tree's mission is to advance the work of our authors. By working with the best researchers and educators worldwide, we strive to be the premier provider of innovative publishing, in-demand events, and inspired professional development designed to transform education to ensure that all students learn.

The mission of the National Association of Elementary School Principals is to lead in the advocacy and support for elementary and middle level principals and other education leaders in their commitment for all children.